" _Drivin_
Machine ~~describes important ways you can improve the~~
safety, reliability, and efficiency of your car. "

- Dan Miller, executive director
American Driver Education Resource Center

" **The Green Machine** _is a clear, concise, and easy-to-read book. It belongs in the personal library of all drivers, both new and experienced._ "

- Byron Briton, executive vice-president
Driving School Association of the Americas

" **The Green Machine** _emphasizes both safety and economical car care with an awareness of good conservation. I highly recommend it!_"

- John Vacek, president
Apple Resources

" **The Green Machine** _is an easy-to-read guide to easy, practical, effective things we can all do to make driving a car safer, more enjoyable, less hassle, and less polluting._"

- Dr. John R. Dixon, P.E.
Professor Emeritus of Mechanical Engineering
University of Massachusetts at Amherst

" **The Green Machine** is an excellent book, easy to read, and containing a wealth of information and tips about operating a car more economically and with less impact on the environment."

- Dan Keegan, editor
the Driver Education Guide to Resources

" **The Green Machine** provides concise, understandable - and most importantly - usable information in a format that makes it a breeze to find what you're looking for."

- John Cummata, president
Financial Independence Network Limited

" **The Green Machine** is a very informative book on safe driving, preventive maintenance, and environmental protection. Using this book will save you money, keep your car running longer, and help our environment. I highly recommend it!"

- Ed Bichard
Las Vegas Driving School

" Road safety is a function of a driver and a car acting together in traffic. **The Green Machine** shows us clearly how we can make the car part of this team work as safely and efficiently as possible. Every responsible driver should know what is in this book."

- David Baker, vice-president
Road Safety Educators Association

*" The two weakest links in our driver education program are mechanics and preventive maintenance. Every driving school and driver should have a copy of **The Green Machine**."*

- Darrell D. Cyr
Cry's Driving School

---

*"**The Green Machine** is a delightful book with wonderful easy to read paragraphs, well illustrated and contains an abundance of information."*

- Graham R. J. Fryer
Driving Magazine

---

*"Keeping your car running better and polluting less is only the beginning. **The Green Machine** can help you drive your car for a long time, ultimately avoiding the premature disposal of a ton and a half of metal, plastic, and glass. This is a unique and essential guide to environmentally responsible driving."*

- Peter A. Ciullo
author of **Save Big Money On A New Car**

---

*" **The Green Machine** emphasizes the relationship between maintenance and safety in a text that is both educational and easy to read. This book should be in every driver's glove compartment."*

- Charles F. McDonald, Jr. executive director
Safety and Health Council of NC

The Green Machine

Drive A Safe, Thrifty, & Environmentally Friendly Car

Jim Gaston

Return Policy

If you are not satisfied for any reason, return this book in good condition along with the sales receipt to the place of purchase for a complete refund.

CoNation Publications
SAN 297-4029
703-G Ninth Street
Durham NC 27705

Printed in the United States of America

Cover Design by Robert Howard

P-Catalog In Publication Data:
Gaston, Jim
The Green Machine
Drive A Safe, Thrifty &
Environmentally Friendly Car
224 p.   21 cm.   Includes Index.
ISBN 1-879699-25-7 (Softcover)
ISBN 1-879699-26-5 (Hardcover)
1. Automobile: Maintenance & Repair
2. Automobile Driving 3. Consumer Education
I. Title.TL152.G   1995   629.28
LC Catalog Card Number: 94-070176

WARNING - DISCLAIMER

This book is based on generally accepted procedures for operating, maintaining and repairing a car. These procedures may differ depending on the particular car or situation involved.

The reader must use caution and consult the owners manual, shop manual, or a trained technician whenever necessary. Improper operation, maintenance, or repairs may cause serious injuries or car damage.

The information contained in this book is accurate and complete to the best of our knowledge. However, the publisher and author specifically disclaim any and all liability for accident, injury, or other loss and risk incurred as a direct or indirect consequence of the advice, recommendations, or information presented in this book.

Consult the owners manual, shop manual, or a trained technician for specific maintenance and repair recommendations about your car. Be sure you understand all procedures completely and follow safety guidelines carefully before starting any repair or maintenance procedure.

Safety Is No Accident !

About The Author

Jim Gaston, the Car Care Professor, earned a mechanical engineering degree from North Carolina State University and graduated from both the North Carolina Division of Motor Vehicles and National Safety Council Instructor Development Courses. He is the author of several other car care books and hosts the weekly call-in radio program **"Car Keys"**.

My goal is to help you have a long and happy relationship with your car. I hope you enjoy this book and keep your car running safely for many years. Drive carefully.

- Jim Gaston
the Car Care Professor

CoNation Publications offers a wide selection of books, audio tapes, computer programs, and video tapes on car care. The books are available from your local bookstore or directly from CoNation. An order form is included at the back of this book.

If you would like FREE information about any of these items, send your name and address to CoNation. Don't let your car drive you crazy, CALL or WRITE today!

Drive With Confidence !

Acknowledgements

I would like to sincerely thank everyone who contributed to the production of this book. Your help and advice have improved the material in many important areas.

Those who deserve special recognition for their professional help are: Jack Dixon, Dan Miller, Chip McDonald, Byron Briton, John Vacek, Dan Keegan, John Cummata, Ed Bichard, David Baker, Darrell Cyr, Graham Fryer, and Peter Ciullo.

Robert Howard patiently designed a beautiful cover. Susan Remkus helped with the task of proofreading the complete text. I specially want to thank Dan Poynter, who provided so much helpful advice and encouragement.

I would like to thank my students, who challenged me in many ways and helped me learn the art of effective communication.

Finally my wife, Jo-C, who shared my dream and contributed some of the artwork in this book.

Dedication

This book is dedicated to my daughter, Jamie. I hope she will grow up to drive safely in a cleaner world.

Jim Gaston
the Car Care Professor

Table Of Contents

Chapter 3 Each Week 35

Chapter 4 Every Two Months 55

Chapter 5 Every Six Months 69

Introduction

There are basically two types of car owners: those who drive till something breaks and those who do preventive maintenance. The goal of this book is to illustrate the advantages of preventive maintenance. Your car will be safer, more economical, and environmentally friendly when you practice safe driving habits and car conservation.

Spending time and money to keep your car in safe driving condition is the smart way to drive. Car conservation will help your car last longer, start easily, operate more efficiently, go farther on each gallon of gasoline, reduce dangerous pollution, and decrease the overall cost-per-mile. You can schedule the service to your car at convenient times and visit the mechanic of your choice.

Safe Driving

If you neglect the basic maintenance of your car, you increase the chance of being involved in a collision or having a road-side breakdown. In addition to the danger or inconvenience this presents, you will spend much more time and money having repairs done and may not have a choice as to parts and repair facilities. Fortunately, most collisions and road-side breakdowns can be prevented with safe driving habits and car conservation.

Time vs. Mileage

Safe driving starts with car conservation. This book is based on general guidelines for average driving conditions of 1000 to 1500 miles a month. You may be accustomed to using mileage to determine when to do the maintenance on your car. I recommend using time because it is easier to schedule and remember.

Calculating maintenance on the basis of miles driven depends on the amount of highway miles or city miles driven. Even a car which is driven very little needs regular maintenance. Whichever system you choose, miles or time, just do it. Your car will last longer and be more reliable.

Car Conservation

Car conservation means driving safely, reducing pollution, making your car last longer, and preventing a roadside breakdown. You can recycle many automotive fluids and parts, which not only helps the environment, but can save you money. Buying remanufactured parts or retread tires are other ways to recycle car parts. Any part of the car which cannot be recycled should be disposed of properly. If you have any questions, call a local auto store or the nearest recycling center.

Refer to the owners manual for the specific maintenance needs of your car.

A Green Machine

Is there really a **Green Machine**? Probably not. Any car or truck on the road today can endanger lives, costs too much money, and cause pollution. However, when you make your car as safe, thrifty and environmentally friendly as possible, you are driving a **green machine.**

Safety First

Safety is paramount when it comes to cars. If you do not arrive at your destination in one piece, not much else matters. Unfortunately, the marketing geniuses at all the auto companies continue to entice us with high tech gadgets to guarantee our safety. Most of these items, however, are only supplemental to the basic safety item in the car (you). Safe drivers do not rely on technology to solve driving emergencies, they anticipate dangers and react accordingly.

Save Money

Cars consume money. They are expensive to purchase, insure, maintain, and operate. Fortunately, learning about car conservation will help you keep your car operating reliably for many years and can save you thousands of dollars. Even if you trade cars every few years, car conservation will help you get more for your trade-in because your car will be in better shape, and therefore more valuable.

Reduce Pollution

Unless you walk or ride a bicycle, getting from one place to another causes pollution. Cars, buses, trains, planes... if it has wheels and a motor, it causes pollution. How can you reduce pollution? You can carpool or use public transportation, when possible. When you drive, there are many ways you can help reduce pollution. How you drive is very important and this book will help you learn how to drive green. Practicing car conservation will ensure that your car operates efficiently, using as little fuel as necessary and producing fewer harmful gases.

Drive Green

You might not own a green machine, but you can take some steps to make your car safer, thrifty, and environmentally friendly. Reconsider other forms of transportation, such as a bicycle or public buses, as they become more common in your area. However, as long as you own and drive a car, become a car conservationist and drive with confidence. Drive Green!

The best way to keep your car running safely for a long time is to become a car conservationist.

Before Driving

When you drive a car every day, it becomes somewhat automatic. You hop in the car, start the engine, and off you go. There are some easy things you can do before you start to drive to improve the safety of your car and reduce pollution.

These tips are easy and quick. They do not require any tools and only a few minutes of your time. Each of these important safety tips can reduce your chance of being involved in a collision or damaging your car. They just might save your life or the life of someone you love.

Safety Is No Accident.

Plan Ahead

Where are you going? What is the best way to get there? Can you carpool with friends or take the bus? Have you considered walking or riding a bike? Do you really need to go today? These questions can help you plan your trip wisely and avoid problems down the road.

Never underestimate the possible delays in driving. If you plan ahead and allow yourself a few extra minutes, you can avoid becoming impatient and taking unnecessary chances while driving. Don't be in a hurry to have a collision.

Make A List

Make a list of the places you are going, the times you must be there, and plan ahead for traffic conditions. Avoid rushing from place to place, unnecessary driving, and heavy traffic areas; these expose you to more dangers on the road, place extra stress on your car, and cause extra pollution. Most importantly, plan ahead so you can enjoy the trip.

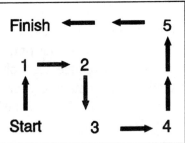

Don't be in a hurry to have a collision or get a speeding ticket.

Loading The Car

Watch the weight in your car. Heavy items or additional passengers will make your car handle differently. The car may be difficult to control while stopping or turning. When your car is full, allow extra stopping distance and slow down before you turn or go over bumps.

Place heavy items near the center of the car so the weight is distributed evenly on all four tires. Place heavy items as low as possible to prevent the car from becoming top-heavy. If your car is top-heavy, it can flip upside down should you need to stop or turn suddenly. Secure heavy items with seat belts, rope, or a tie-down.

Heavy Loads

Heavy loads can damage the suspension or steering system on your car. Drive slower, but allow adequate engine speed. Higher engine RPMs are needed for additional power while going uphill. Do not use overdrive (or 5th gear), unless traveling at a steady speed over 45 MPH.

Unnecessary weight in your car wastes gas and causes extra pollution. Removing 100 pounds of useless stuff from the trunk of your car may enable you to drive an extra 25 miles on a tank of fuel. This saves money and reduces pollution.

Don't overload your car.

Around The Car

Before you get in, quickly check around your car. Look at each tire. Although you cannot properly check the tire inflation just by looking at the tire, you can spot a flat tire. Watch for leaking fluids from your car or any unexpected objects near your car.

If you need to back up, walk around the back of the car before getting inside. Likewise, if you plan to drive straight ahead, approach the car from the front. Watch out for children's toys, pets, glass bottles, rocks, anything that can damage the tires or underside of the car.

Preflight Check

Before a pilot gets into the airplane, they do a "walk-around" preflight inspection. They walk around the plane inspecting important parts, including the tires, engine oil level, and fuel quantity. If we treated our cars with the same tender loving care, they would certainly last longer and be safer vehicles of transportation.

Before you get in, check around the car.

Windows

Would you drive your car blindfolded? No, of course not! Are you driving with dirty windows? If you cannot see clearly, you are more likely to have a collision (or cause one). Tinted windows help reduce heat inside the car, but they can also reduce your visibility, especially at night. In some areas dark tinted windows are illegal. If you have tinted windows, be sure to check carefully before turning or backing up.

You can use the wipers to clean the windows, but they might still leave some dirty spots. At least once a week, clean the inside and outside of the windows using a good glass cleaner or some ammonia and vinegar mixed with water. Newspaper can be used for wiping the glass clean without streaks. This is a good way to reuse old newspaper.

Fog

Fog is another way your vision may be blocked. Use a towel or clean rag to wipe the fog from interior windows. Then turn the heater to HOT, fan to LOW and DEFROSTER. You can also turn the air conditioner ON at the same time to help remove moisture from the air inside the car. Fog is most likely to appear on dirty windows, so keep the windows clean to have a safer car.

Special cleaners which help keep the windows clean on the outside and prevent fog on the inside are available at your local auto stores. Be sure the windows are very clean before applying these cleaners and do not apply too much. Follow the directions supplied with the cleaner for the best results.

Clean windows mean safer driving.

Doors

Keep your car doors locked. Always take your car keys with you and lock the doors when you park the car. Remove valuables from your car or put them in the trunk (out of sight). This does not ensure that your car will not be stolen, but it will certainly make a thief think twice. Special anti-theft devices are available; however, the best and least expensive system is a locked door.

When you get into the car, keep all the doors locked, too. A locked door is less likely to be opened accidentally and will also prevent intruders from entering your car. You cannot be too careful these days, and it certainly helps to keep the doors locked.

Locked Out

What if you get locked out of your car? Some people hide a spare key in a secret place on the car, but anyone who finds it could drive off. Other people keep a spare key in their pocketbook, but if someone steals the pocketbook, they could also steal the car. What should you do? First, keep a spare car key at your home in a safe place. Second, find the "key code" stamped on your car key and keep this information in your wallet and on the car title document at home. You can then have a spare key made at a local dealership or locksmith if you get locked out. Only as a last resort or in emergency situations should you attempt to pick the lock or break into the car. This can cause expensive damage to the car.

Keep the doors locked. Know your "key code."

Loose Objects

Loose objects inside the car can be a dangerous distraction. When you make a sudden turn and a cup of hot coffee spills onto your lap, you might end up suddenly parked against a telephone pole. Put loose objects in the back seat or trunk. Secure all heavy items with a seat belt or rope. Special cargo tie-downs are available at auto stores. Do not put anything near the rear window; it can block your vision or hit you in the back of the head if you stop suddenly.

Avoid Distractions

The strangest things seem to happen at the worst time, often causing collisions. Keep your mind on driving and avoid dangerous distractions. Stop the car before catching the bug flying around inside your car or dialing the number on your cellular phone. You do not want to be zooming down the highway at 55 MPH with your mind on something else.

Secure all loose objects.

Seat & Head Restraint

Before you start the engine, adjust your seat. You should be able to reach the pedals easily and see out the windows. If the seat is too low, sit on a firm cushion. Some cars have an adjustable steering wheel. If so, adjust the steering wheel to easily see the instrument panel. Do not adjust the seat, head restraint or steering wheel while driving.

The head restraint can prevent serious neck injuries in case of an accident. If the head restraint is adjustable, position the top of the restraint to the top of your ears or slightly higher. Do not drive with your head touching the head restraint.

The top of the head restraint should be adjusted slightly above the tops of your ears.

Power Seats

Power adjusting seats can be fun to play with and a great convenience; however, they are not very economical. They are expensive to purchase and when they break, they usually get stuck in an uncomfortable position and cost hundreds of dollars to repair. Manual seats and a pillow are much more practical.

Pedals

Check the pedals before you start the engine and begin driving. You can determine some problems by the feel of the pedal. If you have a problem with your car, it is always better to find out before you are driving down the road.

Brake Pedal

Press the brake pedal three times, then hold it down. It should feel firm and there should be room to slide your left foot under the pedal. If it slowly sinks toward the floor, there may be a leak in the brake system. If the pedal is soft or spongy, there may be air in the system.

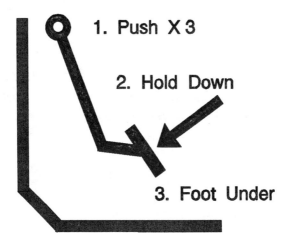

1. Push X 3

2. Hold Down

3. Foot Under

If you have power brakes, the brake pedal may drop slightly as the engine starts; this is normal.

Clutch Pedal

The clutch pedal should have a little "play" or looseness at the top position. The pedal should move down about 1 to 2 inches before additional resistance is felt (when the clutch pedal is actually being depressed). Easy adjustments to remove excessive play in the clutch are recommended and will help make the clutch last much longer. Refer to *Chapter 5 - Manual Clutch*, for more information.

Fuel Pedal

If the car has a carburetor engine and the engine is cold, press the fuel pedal once before you start the engine to set the automatic choke. The car should start easily when you turn the key to START. If the car has a fuel injected engine or the engine is warm, you should not need to press the fuel pedal to start the engine.

Do not pump the fuel pedal; this will flood the engine, waste fuel, cause pollution, and damage the expensive catalytic converter.

All the pedals should move easily. If a pedal begins to make noise or is hard to press, lubricate the pedal hinge point or adjust the linkage.

Remove any objects on the floor which may get in your way when you press the pedals.

Mirrors

Your car should have a center and two outside mirrors (one on each side). If not, have them installed. The mirrors from the car dealerships are the most expensive, but will look much better and be easier to install. Less expensive mirrors are available at local auto stores.

Adjust the mirrors, if necessary, to see traffic behind your car and on each side. Use the mirrors to quickly check the traffic conditions before you turn or stop. Do not, however, rely solely on the mirrors. Turn your head to check the blind spots before making any lane changes.

Blind Spots

You have two blind spots: near the right and left rear corners of the car. You must turn your head and quickly glance to the appropriate side before making a turn or changing lanes, otherwise, you may cause a collision. Never drive in another car's blind spot. Speed up or slow down to avoid driving near the rear of another vehicle.

Check your blind spots before turning.

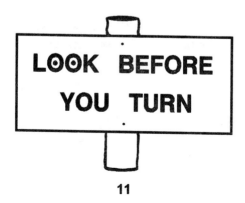

11

Seat Belts

Seat belts, when worn properly, are proven to be the best life saving device available for any collision, in all cars. One reason fewer people died in automobile accidents last year, despite more cars and more miles driven, was increased use of seat belts.

Both the lap belt and shoulder harness are needed for adequate protection.

Wear your seat belt and have all passengers buckle up, too. It is the law in most states. The seat belts should be snug, but not so tight as to be uncomfortable. Children should be buckled in a safety seat. Be sure the safety seat is properly fastened in the right direction with the seat belt.

Airbags

Many new cars are equipped with airbags, but you must still wear the seat belt. If you are thrown out of the driver's seat, an airbag cannot protect you. Airbags are only a supplement to the seat belt and may not inflate in side or rear end collisions. Safety seats for children should not be used in the front passenger seat is the car is equipped with dual air bags.

Seat belts save lives. Buckle Up!

Parking Brake

When you park your car, use the parking brake. Always apply the parking brake firmly. If you set the parking brake gently, you might drive off with the brake partially engaged. This will cause unnecessary brake pad wear and can damage the brake system.

On some cars, using the parking brake also adjusts the rear brake pads. If you seldom use the parking brake, the rear brake may not operate correctly.

Cars With A/T

If your car has an automatic transmission, it is important to set the parking brake properly. Stop the car. While you are still pressing the brake pedal, set the parking brake firmly and shift into Park (P). Then release the brake pedal. When you get ready to leave, press the brake pedal and shift into Drive (D) before releasing the parking brake. This easy technique can prevent damage to the transmission.

If you forget to set the parking brake, the car might roll and bind the locking pin in the transmission. When you try to shift gears, the shifting lever will not move easily, causing damage to the transmission. Using the parking brake properly every time you park your car will help prevent collisions and make the transmission last longer.

Apply the parking brake firmly each time you park the car.

Logbook

Written records are a very important part of good car care. Why? First, keeping a logbook will help you remember to do the maintenance and remind you when it was last performed. Second, written records are evidence that the maintenance was done, in case you need warranty work. Third, the logbook can help increase the resale value of your car and make it easier to sell. The logbook shows that proper maintenance was done.

Write It Down

Every time work is done on the car, write down the date, mileage, work done, cost (list parts and labor separately), who did the work, and the shop invoice number. Avoid general entries which do not tell exactly what was done to your car, for example: *30,000 Mile Service*. It is much better to write down: *Replaced air filter, fuel filter, sparkplugs; adjusted belt tension; rotated tires; checked hoses.*

The **Car Care Logbook** is available from your local bookstore or CoNation Publications. It contains easy to follow checklists and helpful car conservation tips. Write to CoNation for FREE information about the many great car care products.

A car conservationist should keep a LOGBOOK of all maintenance and repairs.

Winter Driving Tips

Cold weather driving demands special attention. Simple problems during warm weather can be very inconvenient or dangerous during winter. Avoid traveling alone or at night during cold weather. Allow extra stopping distance and drive slower when road conditions might be slippery. Bridges and shady spots usually collect snow and ice first and become dangerous.

Fill 'er Up

Refill the fuel tank when it gets half empty. Water condenses on the inside of an empty fuel tank and can cause fuel system problems. A full tank is less likely to have water condensation and prevents running out of fuel.

Avoid using fuel additives to remove water from the fuel. These additives may contain methanol, which can cause other fuel system problems if used frequently.

Clean The Windshield

If snow or ice is in the forecast, park in the garage or cover your windshield to protect it from freezing. Use care when removing the snow or ice to avoid damage to the car. Do not use hot water to remove the ice. This can damage the windshield. Buy a plastic ice scraper and keep it in your car for cleaning the windshield.

Window Cleaning Fluid

Use an approved additive for the window washer fluid to prevent the fluid from freezing. Premixed window washer fluid is available at all auto stores.

Do not use radiator antifreeze in the window washer system. It can damage the exterior of the car.

Carbon Monoxide Alert

Carry warm clothes, a blanket, and some food in the car during the winter. If you get stranded it may be safer to stay in the car until help arrives; however, do not leave the motor running for more than 15 minutes each hour. Exhaust gases, which contain carbon monoxide, can seep inside the car and cause you to become sick or die. Carbon monoxide gas is colorless, tasteless, and odorless, but extremely poisonous. If you feel nauseous, dizzy, or sick, roll down a window to get some fresh air.

Use extra caution when driving in cold weather.

Things To Do Before Driving

1. Clean the car windows inside and out. Use a good glass cleaner and newspaper.

2. Make a copy of your car key to keep at home in a safe place. Find your "key code" and keep it in your wallet and on the car title.

3. Adjust the head restraint. The top of the restraint should be near the tops of your ears.

4. Check the brake pedal. Press it three times and hold. You should be able to put your left foot under the pedal.

5. If a pedal squeaks, spray the hinge points with a lubricant.

6. Adjust the mirrors. Install a right side mirror.

7. Wear seat belts. Check child safety seats for proper installation.

8. Set the parking brake firmly when you park.

9. Keep a logbook.

10. Prepare for winter driving. Put warm clothes, blanket, food in the car. Buy an ice scraper for the windows. Keep the fuel tank at least half full.

Additional Items For Your Car:

While Driving

How you drive is more important than what you drive. Newer cars might have more safety features, but the most important safety feature ever installed in any car is the driver (YOU). A safe driver will avoid collisions despite the actions of other drivers or hazardous road conditions.

There are easy things you can do while driving to avoid a collision, save money, and prevent harmful pollution. The following driving tips do not require any tools. They are good car conservation tips designed to keep your car running safely for many years.

Safe driving begins with car conservation.

Drive Defensively

Defensive driving is avoiding a collision despite the hazardous road conditions. Watch out for the other drivers who are not paying attention and can cause you to be involved in a collision. Keep your distance from big trucks, fast cars, or any vehicle which appears to be in poor condition.

Your #1 priority while driving is to avoid a collision. All other activities, such as arriving on time, looking at the road map, fixing your hair, are secondary. Control the speed and direction of your car and watch out for changing road conditions.

The Most Dangerous Mile

Do you remember how it feels to be warned of danger ahead? Perhaps someone traveling in the opposite direction flashes their headlights, or your radar detector beeps, or you notice yellow flashing lights in the distance. You become very alert, you slow down, you watch for other traffic, you drive defensively. The most dangerous mile of driving is the one immediately ahead of you. After you drive that mile, the next mile instantly becomes the most dangerous. Drive defensively, watch out for danger, arrive safely, and enjoy life.

Avoid Collisions - Drive Defensively

Scanning

How you use your eyes while driving is very important. Keep your eyes moving and concentrate on what you see. Mostly look where the car is going, but also check your mirrors, gauges, blind spots, and surroundings to keep in touch with the driving and road conditions. If you stare at one spot for a long time, you may get sleepy or overlook a dangerous situation.

Blind Spots

All cars have blind spots near the rear of the vehicle. You must turn your head to check the blind spot before changing lanes or turning, otherwise a pedestrian or vehicle may be hiding in the blind spot and you could cause a collision. Do not rely solely on the rear view mirrors, because they cannot reveal objects in the blind spot.

Defensive Driving

Your attitude while driving is very important. If you are tired, upset, angry, distracted or impaired in any way, you will greatly increase your chances of causing a collision. Do not drive a car if you have been drinking or using strong medication. Take a short break, if necessary, to get your mind focused on driving safely and defensively.

Do not drive while under the influence of alcohol, drugs, or strong medication.

Slow Down

Driving fast is a good way to cause a collision or get a speeding ticket. Driving slow can also be dangerous. Both very fast and very slow drivers can cause problems. You should normally move along with the traffic, while observing the speed limit and road conditions.

If you drive very fast, the car burns more fuel and causes unnecessary pollution. If you are involved in a collision, you are more likely to have serious injuries or be killed. A collision or speeding ticket will certainly cause your insurance payments to increase, which is a very significant unnecessary expense.

Best Speed

Your car is the most efficient (highest Miles Per Gallon) when traveling around 50 Miles Per Hour. This means you will be traveling the most distance on the least amount of fuel and producing the least possible pollution. Higher speeds cause the engine to work very hard and burn excessive amounts of fuel. Slower speeds require a lower gear, which also wastes fuel and causes excessive pollution. Always drive according to speed limits and road conditions; however, just remember that 45 to 55 MPH is usually the most efficient speed.

50 MPH is generally the most efficient speed which allows you to travel the most distance on the least fuel and produce the least pollution.

Unnecessary Passing

Before you pass that car ahead, think about it carefully. What will you really gain by passing? What are the risks? Passing is dangerous. Changing lanes, increasing speed, and oncoming traffic are high risks if you only arrive at the next red light a few seconds early. You should maintain a safe following distance and not exceed the speed limit when passing another car.

Overdrive

If you are driving over 45 MPH on flat highways, the engine does not require much power to maintain a steady speed. Many newer cars, both automatic and manual transmissions, have an overdrive gear to help save fuel. Using overdrive at slower speeds or on hilly roads can damage the engine or transmission. Read the section in this chapter about **Engine Speed** and refer to the owners manual for specific information about the correct way to use overdrive in your car.

Some cars with an automatic transmission will shift in and out of overdrive at a certain speed (usually 45 MPH). If this happens, either turn the overdrive OFF or slow down. Overdrive is not really needed unless your car is going faster than 45 MPH.

Enjoy The Trip

Relax and enjoy the trip. Rushing from one place to the next is no way to travel through life. Slow down a little bit and both you and your car will live longer.

Stopping Distance

How quickly can you stop your car? Actually, when you see the danger ahead, you need about one second to decide what to do. Then you need another second to press the brake pedal. During these two seconds, at 40 MPH, you have traveled over 100 feet. It takes about another 100 feet to stop your car. At 55 MPH, double these distances. On wet or icy roads, it might take even longer to stop your car, even with Anti-Lock Brakes!

Anti-Lock Brakes (ABS) do not always reduce the stopping distance of your car. They do provide better control during braking.

Two Second Rule

Forget the one-car-length-for-every-10-MPH method of calculating adequate distance in front of your car. It is too complicated to calculate accurately. Instead, allow at least two-seconds of following distance. When the car in front of you passes some fixed point, count "One Thousand One, One Thousand Two," then you should be at the same spot. This method works at any speed, because at higher speeds you need more distance to count two seconds. Add more seconds for other dangerous conditions, such as a large truck, a motorcycle, bad weather, or poor visibility.

One Thousand One, One Thousand Two

Avoid Tailgaters

Do not follow closely behind other cars. When someone is following too closely behind you, slow down and allow extra space in front of your car. The tailgater will probably pass, but in case you need to stop, do so gently to avoid a rear end collision.

Maintaining adequate stopping distance will help you avoid many collisions and will also prevent unnecessary wear on the brakes, tires, and suspension parts of your car. You will save money and extend the life of your car by being a safer driver.

Headlights

Use the headlights (low beam) when you drive, even in the daytime. Many collisions are caused when someone simply fails to see the other car. Headlights make your car more visible and safer. Most states require motorcycles and school buses to drive with the headlights ON for safety.

Lights OFF

Be sure to turn the lights OFF when you park the car; otherwise, the battery will be drained. Most cars have a warning buzzer to indicate when the lights are ON and the ignition switch is OFF. If you do not have such a buzzer, you can buy one at the auto store and have it installed.

Drive with the headlights ON for safety. Be sure to turn them OFF when you park the car.

Gauges & Warning Lights

Check the oil pressure light when you start the engine. It should come ON when you turn the key to the ON position (before the engine starts), but go OFF as soon as the engine starts. If either the Oil Pressure or Engine Temperature light comes ON while you are driving, stop the car and turn the engine OFF. Serious damage can occur in a few minutes.

Scanning

Keep your eyes moving while you drive. This is called scanning. Mostly look where the car is going, but remember to check the rear view mirrors, instruments, gauges, and warning lights often. Don't just look at items, but think about what you see and what it means. Scanning will help you remain alert while driving.

Daydreams

Keep your mind on driving and on the changing road conditions. Never look at any one item for more than a few seconds and avoid daydreaming. Pay close attention to the speed of the car and amount of fuel available. Use extra caution when driving at night or after eating a heavy meal. Drivers who fall while driving cause many collisions each year.

Keep your eyes moving to help remain alert.

Horn

Some people use the horn more than others, and that's OK. Do not be afraid to use the horn to warn others or get their attention. No one should get upset with a friendly " Beep-Beep." You might want to refrain from a longer " Beeeeeeeeeeeeep," especially in a strange neighborhood.

Keep a finger on the horn button while you drive and use it to avoid a collision. Use courtesy and common sense to avoid upsetting other drivers. There is enough stress out on the highways without having everyone honking at each other. Test the horn at least once a week to be sure it works properly. Do not wait for a dangerous situation to arise, only to find out the horn is broken.

"Beep-Beep" is OK

Steering Wheel

Turn the steering wheel slowly and only when the car is moving. Fast turns, especially at high speeds, can cause the car to go out of control or flip over. Turning the steering wheel when the car is stopped, called dry-steering, can damage both the tires and steering system.

No Sharp Turns

Do not turn the steering wheel all the way to the right or left. If you turn the wheel until it stops, immediately turn it back in the opposite direction, about a quarter turn. This will relieve excess pressure on the steering system and help avoid unnecessary damage. Be careful not to hit a bump while turning, which can damage the wheel alignment.

Locked Steering Wheel

The steering wheel is locked when you remove the keys. You may need to press a special button to remove the key, or push the key IN as you turn it to the OFF position. When you insert the key, it sometimes is hard to turn. Try rotating the steering wheel slightly to the right or left, while turning the key gently.

Do not dry-steer. Turn the steering wheel only when the car is moving.

Engine Speed

The engine is designed to operate between a minimum and maximum speed. The minimum speed is called idle, just fast enough to keep the engine running smoothly without wasting fuel. Most cars idle at about 800 Rotations Per Minute (RPM). The maximum engine speed is called the Redline; a faster speed can cause the engine to fly apart. Most gasoline cars have a redline of about 6000 RPMs; diesel engine have a lower redline of about 4500 RPMs.

Never exceed the engine redline limit.

Best Engine Speeds

Between 2000 and 3000 RPM is the normal operating range for most engines. Lower RPMs, around 2000 RPM, can be used when driving at a constant speed or going downhill. Higher RPMs, around 3000 RPM, may be needed when going uphill or accelerating. If your car does not have a tachometer (engine speed indicator), you can have one installed for about $50. Tachometers can be useful for monitoring the engine speed, even on a car with an automatic transmission.

Lugging

Lugging the engine is very bad and can damage the engine. Lugging is when you drive with a very low engine speed, but are pressing the fuel pedal hard. Lugging causes the engine to rattle, ping, or vibrate. Lugging damages the engine and causes unnecessary pollution. If you drive an automatic transmission, press the fuel pedal down slowly to shift into a lower gear (higher RPM). If you have a manual transmission, shift down into a lower gear, when necessary.

Low engine speeds do not always produce low fuel consumption or less pollution.

Fuel Pedal

Move the fuel pedal slowly and gently. Avoid speeding up quickly, only to stop suddenly. This wastes fuel and causes unnecessary wear on the transmission, brakes, tires, and suspension parts. Take it easy out there on the highway and take it easy on your car if you want it to last a long time. Jackrabbit starts also cause excessive pollution because the fuel and air do not mix or burn completely.

Maintain a constant vehicle speed, when possible.

Cruise Control

Cruise control can be a money saving option if you drive mostly highway miles at a constant speed. Use the cruise control to maintain a steady speed when you are traveling over 50 MPH on relatively open, flat highways. Do not use cruise control in crowded traffic conditions, mountainous terrain, or when your visibility is limited.

Using cruise control while driving on open highways can increase the fuel economy or Miles Per Gallon (MPG) of your car by adjusting the position of the fuel pedal to maintain a steady car speed. A steady speed conserves energy and fuel and will help keep your car running great. Burning less fuel in the engine means less pollution is produced. Proper use of the cruise control can also help you avoid a speeding ticket.

Move the fuel pedal slowly to help conserve fuel and reduce pollution.

Clutch Pedal

If you drive a manual transmission car, learn how to shift gears properly. It takes practice and each car is slightly different. Learn to press the clutch pedal, shift the gear selector, and release the pedal gently while applying just the right amount of pressure to the fuel pedal. When you do it right, you'll know it.

Riding The Clutch

Keep your foot OFF the clutch pedal, except to shift gears. Never drive with your foot touching the pedal, called riding-the-clutch. This can quickly damage the clutch and involve expensive repairs.

Never hold the car in position on a hill by using the clutch pedal; use the brake pedal instead. When you stop the car, press the clutch pedal and brake pedal, shift into neutral (N), and then release the clutch pedal. Holding the clutch pedal down for a long time (more than one minute) can damage the clutch release bearing. It is not easy to start a manual transmission car on a steep incline, but with a little practice, you can do it.

Keep your foot OFF the clutch pedal.

Brake Pedal

Use gentle pressure on the brake pedal for smooth stops. Avoid sudden stops by driving slower or allowing more stopping distance in front of your car. Sudden stops cause unnecessary brake pad wear and can damage the metal disc or drum. Hard braking can also cause the car to go out of control or flip over.

Downhill Braking

Use extra caution when going down a long steep hill. When you use the brakes for a long time, they can get very hot and begin to fade, or lose their ability to stop the car. It is safer to slow down and downshift the transmission to help maintain a slower speed. If the car has a manual transmission, shift from 5th gear to 4th gear. For automatic transmissions, shift from overdrive to 3rd gear (or 3rd gear to 2nd gear).

Do not downshift when the car is going fast or allow the engine to exceed the redline limit.

Things To Do While Driving

1. Drive defensively.

2. Slow down.

3. Use the two second rule.

4. Drive with the headlights ON.

5. Install a headlight warning buzzer to prevent damage to the battery.

6. Check the Oil Pressure Light each time you start the engine.

7. Turn the steering wheel only when the car is moving.

8. Do not lug the engine.

9. Maintain a constant speed when possible.

10. Keep your foot OFF of the clutch pedal.

11. Avoid sudden stops.

Additional Items for your car:

Each Week

Good car conservation saves time and money. Quick and easy adjustments help keep your car running great, reduce pollution, and can prevent major problems. For example, it is easy to add a little oil to the engine. However, if the engine runs out of oil, it's ruined. It is easy to check the air pressure of the tires, but under-inflated tires will wear out quickly and waste fuel. The following weekly checks are quick and easy. However, they are very important and can help you spot possible trouble, before it's too late. Check these items each week or before a long trip.

Car conservation is less expensive and much easier than any major repair.

Oil

Oil is the lifeblood of the engine. It not only lubricates the moving parts inside the engine, but also cleans and cools the engine. Without oil, the engine will overheat, seize-up, and be severely damaged. The owners manual will tell you which type of oil you should use in your car. Synthetic oils and additional oil additives are not needed for most cars.

Dipstick

Use the dipstick to check the oil level in the engine. Be sure the car is parked on a level surface and turn the engine OFF. Remove the dipstick, wipe it clean, and replace it. Remove the dipstick once again to check the oil level. Add more oil, if necessary, to reach the maximum level.

Do not overfill above the maximum level or drive the car when the oil is below the minimum level. One quart of oil will raise the level from minimum to maximum on most cars. If the oil level is low, check the oil filter and drain plug for a leak.

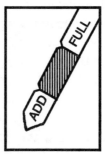

Maintain the engine oil near the FULL level, but do not overfill.

Viscosity

Viscosity indicates the thickness of the oil. The engine needs a thicker oil in the summer and thinner oil in winter. Thicker oil has a higher viscosity number. SAE 30 is a standard engine oil; however, many cars need a multi-weight oil such as 10W-40 all year. A thinner 5W-30 oil will allow slightly more fuel economy, but lower engine protection, especially during hot weather. Check the owners manual for specific information about which oil is recommended for your car.

If the owners manual specifies 5W-30 as the preferred year round oil, 10W-30 (or 10W-40) may be a better choice for summer driving. 5W-30 oil could be too thin for hot driving conditions.

Quality

The quality of the oil has to do with the American Petroleum Institute, or API, rating. Current ratings are SH/CF. A gasoline engine requires the "S" rating. The "C" rating is for diesel engines. The quality of the oil is measured by the second letter, for example the "H" in SH. SH oil is better than older SG oil, which replaced SF oil, and so on. Be sure the oil quality used in your car meets or exceeds the recommendations in the owners manual.

The quality of the oil is not determined by the name brand or cost. Check the API rating. SH oil is better quality than SG or SF oil.

Energy Conserving Oils

Some oils have special additives which make them very slippery. These are called energy conserving oils and are highly recommended for all cars. Using this type of oil will increase your fuel economy (more MPG) and reduce pollution.

If you look on the back of the oil container, there will be a round symbol. The API quality rating is at the top, the viscosity in the center, and Energy Conserving (if the oil qualifies) at the bottom of this circle. All the information you need is in one convenient place.

Price

Expensive oil is not always a better oil. Every oil manufacturer claims their oil is the best and provides tests and endorsements to prove it. Check the API ratings on the oil container and shop at discount auto stores for the best oil at the lowest price.

Synthetic Oils

Synthetic oil is an excellent oil and can be used in most engines. It is, however, very expensive and may not be cost effective. Check with your mechanic or dealership before using this type of oil. There are many different types of synthetic oils available. Some are true synthetic oil (no petroleum). Others are petroleum oil which have been refined for a longer time and may have special additives. There are also synthetic blends, which are a mixture of regular oil and synthetic oil. Check the owners manual to determine which type of oil your car needs and avoid mixing different types of oil together.

Extending the oil and filter change intervals beyond six months or 6000 miles can damage the engine or void the warranty.

Oil Additives

All engine oils contain additives which help protect the engine. Adding more additives, such as an oil treatment, or engine treatment, can upset the delicate additive balance and cause engine problems. Any supplement to the engine oil, regardless of the chance for longer life and increased protection and performance, is not recommended.

Frequent oil and filter changes with a good quality petroleum oil is better for both the engine and your pocketbook than using a synthetic oil with extended oil change intervals.

Brake Fluid

Brake fluid transmits the force applied at the brake pedal to the brake pads located at each wheel. Without adequate brake fluid, your car will not stop. Check the level of brake fluid at the reservoir under the hood. Older cars may have a metal container which requires you to remove the top to check the fluid level. Most newer cars have a transparent plastic container so you can easily check the fluid level without removing the cap.

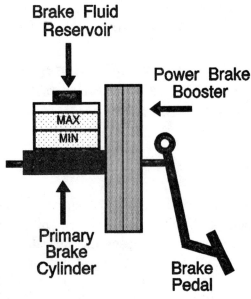

Brake Fluid Reservoir

Power Brake Booster

MAX
MIN

Primary Brake Cylinder

Brake Pedal

Brake Fluid Level

The level should be between the maximum and minimum levels. It will go down very slowly as the brake pads wear; however, any sudden drop in the fluid level indicates a possible leak. Never drive the car when the brake fluid level is below the minimum level. Use clean brake fluid to fill the reservoir to the maximum level.

Clutch Fluid

If your car has a manual transmission, the clutch pedal will operate the clutch with either a wire cable or clutch fluid system. Check for a small reservoir of clutch fluid (or brake fluid) beside the brake reservoir. Check the fluid level, too, and add more fluid when necessary. If you do not find a clutch fluid reservoir, the clutch system uses a wire cable. If you are not sure, ask a mechanic for help.

Do not drive a car when the brake fluid or clutch fluid is below the MINIMUM level.

Radiator Fluid

Radiator fluid circulates between the radiator and engine to maintain the proper engine temperature and prevent overheating. Both a cold engine and very hot engine can damage your car. Radiator fluid is a mixture of water and anti-freeze or coolant. Extra fluid is stored in the expansion tank, located near the radiator.

Radiator Fluid Level

Check the level of radiator fluid in the expansion tank. If you cannot locate the expansion tank, find the small rubber hose under the radiator cap; it is connected to the expansion tank. When the engine is warm, the level of fluid in the expansion tank will be higher because the fluid expands. As the engine cools down, some of the fluid in the expansion tank is syphoned back into the radiator. Do not overfill the expansion tank; this can cause the fluid to spill out as the engine warms up.

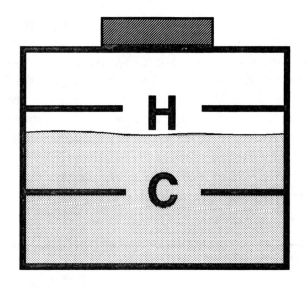

Add a 50:50 mixture of water and coolant to the expansion tank if the fluid level is low. If you need to add fluid often, there is a leak in the system which should be fixed. A pressure test of the radiator system can locate most leaks quickly and easily. Radiator fluid is poisonous, but has a sweet taste. Wipe up spills, repair leaks, and keep the coolant out of reach of children and small animals. A new less poisonous radiator fluid is available for cars, but it cost more, offers lower performance, and requires a special tool for testing.

Do not remove the radiator cap when the engine is HOT. Maintain the radiator fluid level between the HOT and COLD levels.

Window Washer Fluid

One of the most neglected fluids in your car is probably the window washer fluid. Most people do not think to check this fluid until the windows are very dirty and the reservoir is empty. Window washer fluid helps clean the windows and prevents damage to the wipers. Do not drive your car with dirty windows.

Check the level of washer fluid in the reservoir. Plain water can be used in the system, but, it does not clean very well and might freeze in cold weather. Inexpensive premixed washer fluid, which will not freeze, is available at all auto stores. Fill this reservoir so you will be able to clean the windows as needed and remember to check and refill it, as needed.

Use premixed window washer fluid to clean the windows. Refill the reservoir each week or as needed..

Power Steering Fluid

The power steering system allows you to steer your car with less effort and have better control. Power steering fluid circulates between the power steering pump (near the engine) and the steering box (between the front wheels).

P/S Fluid Level

Check the level of power steering fluid in the reservoir near the pump. The reservoir may be part of the power steering pump or a separate reservoir attached to the pump with a hose. A small dipstick may be attached to the bottom of the reservoir cap. Most reservoirs, however, are transparent to allow you to easily check the fluid level. Maintain a level between the minimum and maximum marks. Do not overfill.

Some cars use automatic transmission fluid in the power steering systems. Other cars require a special fluid. Check the owners manual and use the correct type of fluid for your car to avoid damage to the system.

If you do not have enough power steering fluid, the car will be harder to steer and make strange noises when you turn the steering wheel.

Automatic Transmission Fluid

The automatic transmission shifts gears depending on the speed of the engine and position of the fuel pedal. The automatic transmission uses a special fluid to operate both the transmission and clutch. Check the owners manual for the location of the dipstick and inspection method needed for your car.

Dexron (Mercron) and Type F (M2C33-F) are two different types of Automatic Transmission Fluid (ATF). Check your owners manual or ask a mechanic if you are not sure which fluid is needed for your car.

Checking the ATF

Before checking the automatic transmission fluid level, warm up the engine (drive 10 minutes). Park the car in a safe level place and apply the parking brake, but do not turn the engine OFF. Shift the transmission slowly from Park (P) to First (1) and then back to Park (P). Use caution to avoid any moving or hot engine parts and carefully remove the automatic transmission dipstick from under the hood. Wipe it clean and replace it. Remove it again to check the fluid level.

Use caution when checking the ATF level.

Color & Odor

Note both the color and odor of the fluid. Automatic transmission fluid should be pink or red. If it is dark or smells like burnt coffee, have the transmission fluid changed immediately. Additional transmission repairs may also be needed. If the fluid level is low, add a small amount of automatic transmission fluid through the dipstick hole and check the level again.

Dark or burnt automatic transmission fluid indicates damage to the transmission.

45

Tires

Tires are one of the most important, often neglected, parts on your car. Properly maintained tires will save fuel, reduce pollution, provide a comfortable and safe ride, and last several years of normal driving. Tires not properly maintained will wear out quickly, waste fuel, and can cause a collision.

Check the pressure of each tire using an accurate gauge when the tires are cold (less than 5 miles of driving). The recommended tire pressure for your car can be found in the owners manual. The maximum pressure is indicated on the side of the tire. Do not overinflate the tires. The longest tire life, most MPG, and least pollution will be achieved with properly inflated tires. Check the spare tire, too. It may be a special compact tire which requires a much higher pressure.

Air Pressure Gauge

Both the long pencil gauge and round dial gauge are available. Buy an air pressure gauge and keep it in your car or garage, so you can check the air pressure once a week. Avoid very inexpensive gauges which may not be very accurate or durable. If you need to add more air, use a manual pump, 12-volt electric pump, or drive to the nearest service station. Add air to the tire slowly, checking the pressure often, to prevent over-inflation.

Check the tire pressure when the tires are cold or before driving very far. Do not overinflate tires.

Tool Kit

Your car should have a basic tool kit. Below is a general recommended list. Add additional items, if necessary.

1. Owners Manual
2. Flashlight (spare bulb, fresh batteries)
3. Spare Tire
4. Jack
5. Lug Wrench
6. Tire Pressure Gauge
7. Adjustable Wrench
8. Vise-Grip Pliers
9. Screwdrivers (Flat and Star)
10. Jumper-Cables
11. Eye Protection
12. Fire Extinguisher (CO_2, ABC, Halon)
13. Battery Terminal Cleaner
14. Knife
15. Fuses (assorted AMP sizes)
16. Radiator Sealer (powder type)
17. Hose Clamps
18. Electrical or Duct Tape
19. Rubber Hose (1/4 ID X 6 feet)
20. Matches or Lighter
21. Small File
22. Wire Coat Hanger
23. Several Clean Rags

Addition Items:

Your Own Tool Kit

Although you can buy a tool kit for your car, you will usually get better quality parts at less cost if you put together your own kit. Visit your local auto store and ask the salesperson for assistance or suggestions. There are many useful items available today, such as a small rechargeable flashlight which plugs into the cigarette lighter.

Even if you are not mechanically inclined, having some tools might allow someone else to help you in an emergency situation.

First Aid Kit

Your car should also have a basic first aid kit. Below is a general recommended list of items. Add additional items, if necessary.

1. Assorted Sterile Adhesive Strips
2. Aspirin or other pain reliever
3. Soap
4. Insect Repellent
5. Scissors
6. Needle and Thread
7. Razor Blades
8. Safety Pins
9. Salt Tablets
10. Moleskin Adhesive
11. Tape
12. Thermometer
13. Snakebite Kit
14. Sterile Gauze Pads
15. Antacid Tablets
16. Antiseptic Cream
17. Antihistamines
18. Elastic Bandages
19. Matches (Waterproof)
20. Baking Soda (Neutralizes Battery Acid)
21. Special Medication

Additional Items:

Your First Aid Kit

Unlike the tool kit, which you can assemble yourself, a good general first aid kit is usually available for a reasonable cost at most drug stores. You can add any special medications you might require. Be sure to check the first aid kit every six months and replace any damaged items.

Include special medication and a first aid manual in the first aid kit. Write the name and phone number of your doctor, the nearest Poison Control Center, and a relative in the first aid kit.

Lights & Turn Signals

The lights and turn signals are important safety devices. Headlights allow you to see the road and others to see your car. Turn signals should be used *before* you turn to warn others of your intentions. If the lights or turn signals are broken, you are more likely to be involved in a collision.

Check the lights and turn signals to be sure they are working properly. Have someone watch the bulbs as you test each light. When a turn signal breaks, it may blink very fast or not at all. Check for a broken fuse before changing the bulb. If both the bulb and fuse are OK, but the light still does not work, the problem may be a broken flasher under the dashboard. The flasher is inexpensive and easy to change.

Replacing A Bulb Or Flasher

Most bulbs and flashers are also easy to change, once you get to them. The shop manual describes the location of these items and specific instructions. Turn the ignition key OFF before making any electrical repair. Most small bulbs can be removed with a push and turn. Install a new bulb by pushing and turning the opposite direction. Larger bulbs often plug into a socket. Flashers usually plug into the fuse panel. Some electrical connections are covered with special grease to prevent corrosion; do not wipe it off.

Turn the ignition key OFF before making any electrical repair. Include various size (AMP) fuses in the tool kit and learn how to change a fuse.

Clean The Car

A dirty car looks bad and can easily rust. If you do not want to clean the car yourself, go to a full service car wash. A clean car will look great and last longer.

If you clean your own car, follow these easy tips:

1. Avoid direct sunlight. Find a shady spot or wash the car in the late afternoon.

2. Don't waste water. Use a spray nozzle which cuts off when you let go or turn the water OFF, except when needed.

3. Rinse the entire car with clean water before you start washing. This loosens the dirt. Wash the top of the car first and work your way down, leaving the dirtiest sections for last.

4. Do not scratch or rub very dirty spots. Soak the spot with a wet rag for several minutes to loosen the dirt.

5. Use a mild biodegradable soap or car washing liquid that does not contain phosphates or other harmful chemicals.

6. Clean out the drain holes on the bottom of the car doors or body. Clogged drain holes can cause rust.

7. Use special cleaners for vinyl, plastic, or rubber parts. This will restore a beautiful appearance and prevents these parts from cracking.

8. Wash dirt or salt off the underneath sections of the car.

9. Rust spots should be cleaned with sandpaper and painted to prevent the rust from spreading.

10. Do not spray water onto the top of the engine or on any electrical devices.

11. Clean inside the car, too. Throw away the trash and vacuum the carpet or upholstery to remove dirt.

Keep your car clean and paint any rust spots.

Air Conditioner & Heater

The air conditioner system uses a high pressure gas to cool the car. The heater system uses hot radiator fluid to warm the car. If either the air conditioner or heater breaks, you might still be able to drive the car, but it will be much less comfortable.

Run both the air conditioner and heater at least 10 minutes each week (engine running). This keeps the gases and fluids circulating and lubricates the valves, seals, and other internal parts. If you do not use the air conditioner for several months, the high pressure gas can leak out. If you do not use the heater for several months, the radiator fluid in the heater system may become contaminated.

A/C Removes Fog

Running the air conditioner in the winter, along with the defroster, removes moisture from the air and helps prevent fog on the windows. Move the temperature selector to HOT to keep from blowing very cold air. Some newer cars automatically run the A/C for a short time when the defroster is ON.

Run both the air conditioner and heater at least 10 minutes each week, all year long.

53

Things To Do Each Week

1. Check the engine oil level.

2. Which type of oil is needed in your car?
   Viscosity (SAE 30, SAE 10W-40)?
   Quality (API: SH or CF)?

3. Check the brake fluid (and clutch fluid).

4. Check the radiator fluid in the expansion tank.

5. Check the power steering fluid reservoir.

6. Check the automatic transmission fluid.

7. Check the pressure in each tire (spare, too).
   Buy an air pressure gauge for your car.

8. Check the tool kit. Add additional items.

9. Check the first aid kit.

10. Check the lights and turn signals. Keep an
    assortment of different size (AMP) fuses.

11. Clean the car. Paint any rust spots.

12. Run both the heater and air conditioner at
    least 10 minutes.

Additional Items:

Every Two Months

The owners manual might recommend changing the oil every six months or 7500 miles for normal service or three months or 3000 miles for severe service. Some people never change the oil, they just change cars! Changing the oil very often is a waste of money, labor, and oil. Postponing oil changes can cause major engine damage. What should you do? Consider this: changing the oil and filter is easy and inexpensive compared to any engine repair. Good car conservation every two months will help you keep your car in peak efficiency for many years of dependable use.

Changing the engine oil and filter is easy and inexpensive compared to any engine repair.

Oil & Filter

Changing the engine oil and filter is one of the easiest and most important maintenance items. The oil not only lubricates the moving parts inside the engine, but also helps clean and cool the engine. If you forget to change the oil and filter or try to save money by changing the oil less often, you will end up spending a lot of money on engine repairs or a new car. If you want to keep your car running for a long time, change the oil and filter regularly, at least four times each year or once each season.

Helpful Hints

If the engine is cold, run it for several minutes to allow the oil to circulate and warm up. Park the car in a safe level place and turn the engine OFF. Place a large bucket under the engine and remove the oil drain plug. While the oil is draining out, remove the old filter (a filter wrench may be needed). Apply some oil to the rubber O-ring on a new filter and install it correctly. Do not over tighten the new filter.

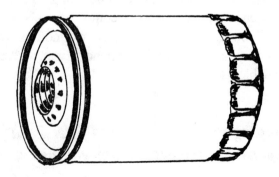

Replace the oil drain plug, using a new gasket or washer. Neglecting to install a new oil plug gasket can cause a small oil leak. Purchase a dozen gaskets at the local dealership and keep them in the car so you can give one to the mechanic when you have the oil changed.

Add the proper amount of clean oil through the oil fill cap on the top of the engine. After changing the oil and filter, start the engine and watch the oil pressure warning light. If it does not go OFF in five seconds, turn the engine OFF and check for leaks. If it does go OFF, allow the engine to run for several minutes, then turn the engine OFF. Check the oil level using the dipstick. Add more oil if necessary, to reach the maximum level, but do not overfill.

Oil Spills

When a large oil tanker spills millions of gallons of oil into the ocean, the environmental impact is easily seen. Every day, smaller quantities of oil are dumped into the environment which can also have a detrimental impact. A teaspoon of dirty engine oil leaking from your car or poured onto the ground can contaminate thousands of gallons of water.

Fix any oil leaks on your car. Allow empty oil containers and the dirty oil filter to drain into a pan overnight. Then pour the oil in with the old oil for recycling. The small amount of oil in empty containers or dirty filters can leak into the ground and pollute underground water. Old engine oil can be recycled at some auto stores or most recycling facilities.

Change the oil and filer regularly. Fix oil leaks and recycle used oil.

Lubrication

All cars need lubrication, although newer cars need less attention than older cars. Suspension parts, hinges, pedals, cables, and other moving parts need a slippery surface to prevent unnecessary wear. If you do not lubricate the car, it will start to squeak and wear out sooner.

Newer cars may have plugs installed where grease fittings should be located. If you want these parts to last longer, ask your mechanic to remove the plugs and install grease fittings, if possible. Then lubricate these parts regularly with a grease gun. Use the type of grease recommended in the shop manual.

Spray lubricants are also useful for some areas. Squeaky pedals or seat springs could use a squirt of oil to make them be quiet. Check the shop manual for lubrication points and recommended grease or lubricants.

Locks & Switches

Do not use oil or spray lubricants in the door locks or ignition switch. Wet lubricants might cause these parts to malfunction. Special dry graphite lubricants are available for these parts, if needed. Follow the directions which come with the lubricants..

Proper lubrication will extend the life of many car parts and prevent annoying squeaks.

Battery

When the battery is being recharged, some of the water inside the battery evaporates. Maintenance free or low maintenance batteries are specially designed to capture this water vapor and return it to the battery. These batteries should seldom need additional water. If the fluid level inside the battery goes down in one or more cells, it may be possible to remove the caps on top of the battery and add some distilled water.

Do not add regular tap water to the battery. It contains minerals or chemicals and will damage the battery.

Make sure the battery is secure. If it falls over, acid can spill or it may start a fire. A red rubber cover should be installed over the positive terminal to prevent any metal object from touching it. Check for corrosion near the battery terminals. Remove any corrosion with sandpaper or a wire brush. Install anti-corrosion washers (available at auto parts stores) to prevent corrosion at the battery terminals.

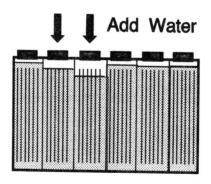

Add Water

Clean The Battery

If the battery gets dirty, clean it. A thin film of dirt and grease on the battery can allow electrical power to slowly drain out of the battery. Wash it with soapy water and baking soda, but be careful not to allow the dirty water to get inside the battery.

Maintenance free batteries need maintenance. Add only distilled water to the battery.

Belts

Belts are used to turn the water pump, alternator, air conditioner compressor, power steering pump, radiator fan, and pollution controls. Most cars have several belts, depending on the options installed; other cars have one long belt which serpentines around every pulley.

Check the tension and condition of the belts. Press firmly on the belt between two of the pulleys. If the pulleys are more than one foot apart, the belt should move about 1/2 inch. If the pulleys are closer together, 1/4 inch is normal deflection. Look for cracked or torn places on the belt and replace any damaged belts.

Adjust Belts

Adjust the tension of the belts by moving one item, such as the alternator, away from the engine. Loosen the pivot bolt and lock nut. Then turn the adjusting bolt, or carefully pull the alternator outward, until the belt is tight. Then tighten the lock nut and pivot bolt. Some newer cars have an automatic belt tension adjuster. Refer to the shop manual for specific belt adjustment instructions.

Push Down   1/2 Inch

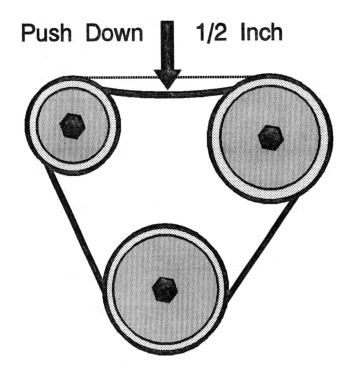

Do not over tighten the belt(s). Belts which are too tight will not last very long. On the other hand, a loose belt will slip and be damaged, too. Belts usually slip when they get wet. Water splashed onto the engine can cause the belts to slip. If the belt slips, tighten it.

Do not use belt dressing or other sprays to stop a slipping belt. Adjust the belt tension according to the shop manual.

Radiator Hoses

Rubber hoses connect the radiator to the engine. There are other radiator hoses connected to the heater system and some engines have other small radiator hoses near the thermostat or engine. Check the hoses visually for leaks, cracks, or other damage when the engine is OFF and cold. Squeeze the hoses in several places. They should feel firm, not soft or brittle.

Hoses should last four to five years. Old hoses may start deteriorating on the inside, even though they still look in good condition on the outside. Replace the radiator hoses before they break to avoid overheating the engine. Refer to Chapter 8 for more information about the hoses.

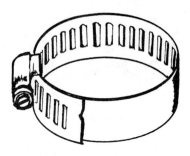

Hose Clamps

If a hose is leaking near the clamp, simply tighten the clamp to stop the leak. Do not, however, over tighten the clamps, which could cut or damage the hose. Always use new clamps when installing a new hose.

Check the radiator hoses for leaks, particularly near each hose clamp.

Steering Wheel Play

Turning the steering wheel moves the front wheels to the right or left. Some looseness is built into the steering system to allow certain steering parts to move freely. If the looseness, or "play," exceeds the normal limit, the steering system becomes unsafe.

Steering Test

There is an easy way to test the steering system. Hold the steering wheel near the top and at the same time look out the window at the front tire. Slowly turn the wheel to the right until the tire starts to move, then stop. Slowly turn the wheel to the left until the tire starts to move in the other direction, then stop. Repeat this back and forth motion, observing how far your hand is moving. Normal steering wheel play is one or two inches. If the play exceeds two inches, the steering system needs to be adjusted or repaired.

WARNING: When doing this test, be careful not to dry steer or cause the tires to scrape on the road. This damages both the tires and steering system. Turn the wheel slowly just enough to cause the tires to begin to move.

Normal steering wheel play is one to two inches.

Seat Belts

Seat belts need very little maintenance. However, you can check the belts to be sure that they are in good shape and working properly. Check each seat belt carefully. Start with the buckle. Fasten and release it several times to be sure it fastens securely. Then inspect the strap or belt; look for signs of wear near the buckle or other connection points. Finally, check the other end of the belt where it attaches to the frame of the car.

Most seat belts are spring-loaded to adjust to different size passengers. Some belts lock in place when you suddenly pull on the belt (inertia type). Other belts lock in place when the car suddenly changes speed (pendulum type). If you have any question about the safety of a seat belt, have it inspected at the local dealership.

Any problem or damage to the seat belt must be repaired according to the shop manual. Do not modify or tamper with the features of the seat belt or any safety device on your car.

Check each seat belt carefully for proper operation.

Fuel Economy

Fuel economy, or the number of miles the car will go on a gallon of fuel, is a measure of the efficiency or condition of the car. A sudden decrease in fuel economy may indicate a simple problem, such as a fouled sparkplug or a dirty air filter.

MPG Ratings

The fuel economy or MPG ratings for a new car is calculated with a standard formula and may not represent actual test results. Your driving habits and the road conditions will greatly affect the actual mileage you will experience. Use the MPG ratings for comparison only.

Calculate MPG

Calculate fuel economy by filling up the fuel tank and writing down the current mileage on the odometer. Do not overfill the tank, which can damage the emission controls or spill fuel. Then drive normally until you need to refill the tank. When you stop to refill the tank, calculate the number of miles you have driven and the number of gallons needed to refill the tank. Divide the number of miles you drove by the number of gallons of fuel needed to refill the tank. This is the Miles Per Gallon or MPG.

Use your logbook to keep accurate records of the date, mileage (odometer), and amount of fuel used in your car.

Use the following outline to make calculations of the MPG quickly and easily. Fill up the tank and write the starting mileage in (1). Drive until you need more fuel. Then fill up again and write the mileage in (2). Calculate the miles driven in (3). Write the number of gallons of fuel used in (4). Calculate the MPG in (5).

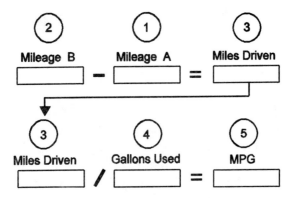

A small decrease in fuel economy can cost you an additional $100 (or more) each year in fuel. It might also indicate the car will not pass the annual exhaust emission test. This can result in expensive repairs to the pollution control items, such as the oxygen sensor or catalytic converter. Maintain good MPG records in your logbook and keep your car running great.

Things To Do Every 2 Months

1. Change the engine oil & filter.

2. Lubricate the car body.

3. Check the battery. Clean terminals or add distilled water, if necessary.

4. Check the engine belts.

5. Check the radiator hoses.

6. Check the steering wheel play.

7. Check each seat belt.

8. Calculate the fuel economy (MPG).

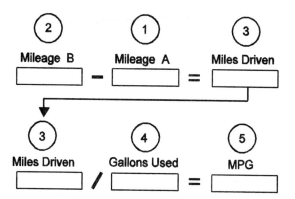

Additional items for your car::

Every Six Months

The spring and fall are good times to give your car a little extra attention. This helps ensure that the car is ready for the hot or cold weather driving conditions ahead. Good car conservation will keep your car running great. Most of these procedures can be divided into two categories: the tires- brakes-suspension inspections and minor engine adjustments. Although these procedures are easy, some require special tools or training. Many repair shops offer free vehicle inspections. If repairs are needed, they can be done by your mechanic.

Regular inspections and minor adjustments can prevent a major expensive repair or roadside breakdown.

Tires

Tires are an important, and expensive, part of your car. Good tire care will save money, increase the life of the tires, and make your car safer. In addition to proper tire pressure (Chapter 3), you need to keep each tire properly balanced and rotated.

Tire Balance

Tires must be balanced so they will spin smoothly at high speeds. Unbalanced tires wobble or hop, which causes excessive tread wear and damage to the steering system. Small metal weights are attached to the wheel rim, usually opposite the tire valve, to balance each wheel.

Rotation

Tires should also be rotated, or moved to a different wheel position, to promote even tread wear. All tires can use a front to back rotating method. Avoid moving radial tires from side to side, as this might damage the tires or cause poor tire performance. Rotating tires also provides an opportunity to visually inspect the brake system and underneath the car.

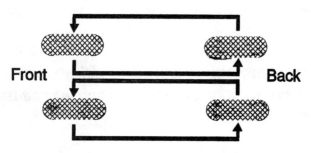

Many tire or brake shops offer free inspection and tire rotation. Balancing is not free, but is recommended at least once a year. If the steering wheel shakes while driving over 45 MPH, definitely have the tires balanced. If the car drives smoothly at highway speeds, it may not be worth paying extra to balance each tire, just rotate them. When shopping for new tires, however, negotiate for free rotation and balancing every six months or 6000 miles to be included in the purchase price or for a small fee.

Steering wheel vibrations (over 45 MPH) are usually caused by an out of balance tire.

Brakes

Inspect the brake system when the tires are rotated. Disc brakes are easier to inspect; you simply need to remove the tire. Drum brakes require a little more effort because you must remove both the tire and brake drum.

Do not breathe the brake lining dust. It may contain asbestos or other dangerous materials.

Brake Inspection

There are three parts to the brake inspection: pad thickness, rotor/drum condition, and leaks in the system. First, check the brake pad thickness. When any part of the brake pad wears down to the minimum thickness, about 1/16 inch, all the brake pads on that axle must be changed. For example, replace all four front brake pads, or all four rear brake pads at the same time, otherwise the car will not stop safely.

Next, check the condition of the brake rotor or drum. Very small scratches are normal and do not require any repair. Large grooves or slight warped conditions can be removed by a process called "turning" which produces a perfectly smooth surface. If the brake pads are replaced before the pads wear out, turning is not usually necessary, but is often recommended. If the brake drum or rotor is cracked or badly warped, it should be replaced. Before you agree to have the drum or rotor turned, compare the cost of turning to a new part; it may only be slightly more expensive to install a new part..

Avoid excessive turning of the drum or rotor. This can remove too much metal and cause it to warp or crack.

Finally, check for leaks in the brake system. Brake fluid will damage the pads and prevent the car from stopping properly. Leaks in the brake system are usually caused because the brake fluid is over two years old and has become dirty or contaminated with water.

Adjusting Brakes

Disc brakes are self adjusting, or in other words the brake pads automatically adjust to compensate for brake pad wear. Drum brakes, however, can get out of adjustment. Driving in reverse and applying the brakes will adjust the brakes in some cars. Other cars adjust the rear drum brakes when you apply the parking brake. Some drum brakes must be manually adjusted. Check the shop manual or ask your mechanic how to adjust the drum brakes on your car.

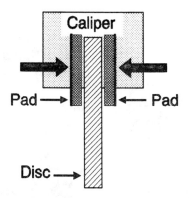

When replacing brake pads, purchase the proper type for your car. Improper pads may cause noise, wear faster, or not stop the car safely.

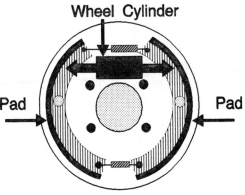

Wheel Bearings

Each wheel has a set of bearings to allow the wheel to turn easily and provide the best fuel economy (highest MPG). Bearings which are properly lubricated and adjusted will last longer and reduce pollution. The bearings are located at the center of the wheel (near the axle) and are lubricated with grease or oil to provide a slippery surface and prevent excessive heat.

Test Wheel Bearings

The wheel bearings should be tested as part of the tire rotation and brake inspection. Raise the wheel off the ground (do not loosen the tire). Grab the tire at the top and bottom and try to shake it and then grab it on the left and right sides and shake it. Some very slight movement is normal; however, if the wheel is loose, the bearing needs to be tightened or replaced. Next, spin the tire forward and backwards slowly and listen for grinding sounds from the bearings.

Lubricating Bearings

Most cars use permanently sealed bearings which do not need additional lubrication. Some cars have regular bearings which need to be cleaned and repacked with fresh grease. Check the shop manual or ask your mechanic to find out which type of bearings are on your car and what service they need. Removing, cleaning, and adding fresh grease to the wheel bearing every two years is good car conservation.

Replacing Wheel Bearings

Bearings will start to make noise when they wear out. Replace the bearings before they break and damage the more expensive axle or wheel housing or cause a collision. Bearings must be installed and adjusted properly. A loose bearing will vibrate or wobble and be damaged quickly. A very tight bearing cannot roll freely and will overheat.

Wheel bearings need adequate lubrication and must be installed correctly. Both a loose bearing and a tight bearing will be damaged quickly.

Shock Absorbers

Shock absorbers are needed for a smooth and safe ride. The springs actually support the weight of the car, but the shock absorbers prevent the springs from bouncing too much. If the shock absorber is located inside the coil spring, it is called a strut.

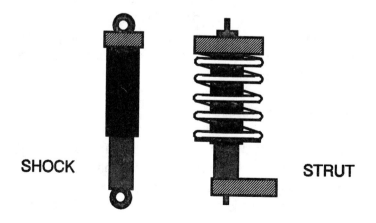

SHOCK   STRUT

75

Testing Shock Absorbers

Testing a shock absorber is very easy. Park the car in a safe level place. Push down hard near one corner of the car and then release suddenly. The car should bounce up, down, then stop as it goes up the second time. If it continues to bounce, the shock absorber is worn out and should be replaced. Repeat this test at each corner of the car. You will also notice the bouncing more and becoming harder to handle the car if the shock absorbers are worn out. Replace all shock absorbers at the same time; however, you can just replace them in pairs: front two, or rear two.

Bounce the car to easily test for worn out shock absorbers or struts.

Inspect Springs

The springs seldom need to be replaced, unless the car was overloaded or driven too fast on very bumpy roads. If the car sits level at a normal height, the springs do not need to be replaced. When replacing the struts, the mechanic will often use the original springs or trade-in the old springs to be used on another car. A visual inspection of the suspension system should be part of the tire rotation and brake inspection.

Replacing Shock Absorbers

Replacing standard shock absorbers is very easy. Simply unbolt the old shock and install the new one. Install new rubber bushings on each shock. Struts, however, are much more complicated and demand special tools and training.

After replacing a strut, the wheel alignment may need to be adjusted. Therefore, arrange strut replacement when you purchase new tires or have a routine wheel alignment to save on labor cost. Refer to the shop manual for specific instructions about the shock absorbers on your car.

Driving with worn shocks or struts can be dangerous, uncomfortable, and cause a collision.

Carburetor

Fuel and air must be mixed in proper proportions so the engine will start easily, run smoothly, and achieve normal fuel economy (MPG). Mixing fuel and air is done with either a carburetor or fuel injection system. The choke is a part of the carburetor, which provides a little extra fuel when the engine is cold.

Carburetor Cleaning

Carburetors can get dirty from normal use. An easy way to clean the carburetor and choke is with a spray can of carburetor cleaner purchased at your local auto store. When the engine is OFF, remove the air filter and follow the directions on the can of spray cleaner. Spray the cleaner thoroughly on both the inside and outside of the carburetor. Spray down into the carburetor to remove varnish or residue buildup. Spray outside the carburetor, especially on the choke and linkage systems, to remove dirt, oil, or crud, which can prevent proper carburetor operation. It is most important to clean the outside of the carburetor. Fuel additives in gasoline help keep the inside of the carburetor clean, but cannot remove dirt on the outside of the carburetor.

Spray clean the carburetor inside and out with carburetor/choke cleaner.

Fuel Injection Cleaners

Fuel injection systems are very reliable as long as the engine computer gets proper electronic inputs and the fuel is clean. All major brands of gasoline contain adequate cleaning additives to prevent clogging of the fuel injectors. If the fuel injection engine starts easily, runs smoothly, and gets normal fuel economy (MPG), additional fuel additives or fuel injection cleaning is not recommended. For more information about fuel injectors, refer to Chapter 7.

Engine Valves

The engine has two types of valves: intake and exhaust. Intake valves allow the fuel and air mixture to enter the engine. Exhaust valves let the burned gases escape out the tail pipe. For many years cars had only one intake and one exhaust valve per cylinder. New cars have multi-valve engines, or more than one intake (or exhaust), valve per cylinder to achieve more efficient operation and lower pollution levels.

Hydraulic or Standard

There are two types of valves found on modern cars: hydraulic and standard. Hydraulic valves are self adjusting and, except for changing of the engine oil, they do not need regular maintenance.

If the engine is equipped with hydraulic valves, no adjustments are needed.

Adjusting Standard Valves

Engines with standard valves should be checked every six months to be sure they are not loose or tight. A loose valve will cause clicking noises from the engine, especially at idle speed. Loose parts banging together will reduce engine performance and eventually cause something to wear or break.

A very tight valve, however, is more dangerous. This valve cannot close completely, which will cause the valve to burn up quickly. Damage to a single valve will require a complete valve job, which is an expensive repair.

Adjusting the engine valves is easy. It requires a feeler gauge (or shims), screw driver, wrenches, and the shop manual. The complete procedure should take about 30 minutes and is usually done when the engine is cold. If the engine has a rubber timing belt, inspect it at the same time.

Both a tight or loose valve can be damaged and cause expensive engine repairs.

Manual Clutch

In Chapter 2 we discussed keeping your foot off of the clutch pedal as much as possible to avoid unnecessary clutch wear. As the clutch wears, however, it is necessary to make adjustments to maximize the clutch life. Fortunately, there is an easy way to test the clutch pedal, which you can do yourself. There should be some play, or free movement, at both the top and bottom of the clutch pedal. Perform the following test in a safe level place.

Clutch Test

With the engine running and car in first gear, measure how far the clutch pedal must be raised (from the fully depressed position) to make the car start to move. Normal play of the pedal from the bottom position is two inches upward.

Then shift into neutral and release the clutch pedal (hold the brake pedal). First, listen for any unusual sounds from the transmission. Carefully press the clutch pedal until you feel some resistance on the pedal. Normal play of the clutch pedal from the upper position is one inch downward.

If you find too much play at either the top or bottom positions, adjust the clutch. Adjusting the clutch is easy and certainly less expensive than replacing the clutch. Proper adjustments will extend the clutch life and reduce the cost-per-mile of owning your car. Refer to the shop manual for specific test and adjustment procedures for your car or ask a mechanic for help.

Normal clutch pedal play is about one inch from the top pedal position and two inches from the bottom.

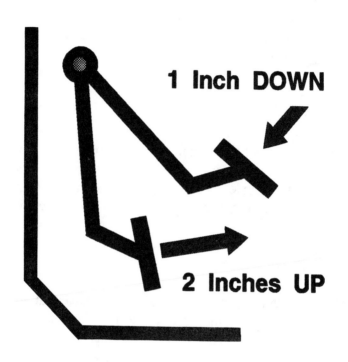

1 Inch DOWN

2 Inches UP

Replacing The Clutch

The life of the clutch is directly related to your driving habits. An average life is 75,000 miles; however, 150,000 miles on one clutch is not impossible. When you replace the clutch, install a new clutch release bearing, too. This inexpensive part is sometimes overlooked and can cause noise or another expensive clutch repair if not replaced along with the new clutch.

Polish The Car

Polish protects the car from sunlight, water, and dirt. It also helps keep your car looking like new. There are a lot of different cleaners, creams, paste, protectors, glazes, and sealants on the market today. However, most are just basically polishes.

Polish Test

The easiest way to determine the condition of your cars exterior is to watch how water beads on the hood. A well rounded water droplet indicates adequate protection. Flat droplets or sheeting action indicates little or no protection.

Liquid Polish

There are several good liquid polishes available that are easy to apply and should last several months (although they claim to last one year). For professional results try a soft polish which does not contain any cleaner. Your local auto store should stock a variety of car polishes. Always wash your car thoroughly before polishing and use clean soft cotton rags.

Avoid using any polish or cleaner with abrasive materials. Although these products remove old wax or dull paint, it might damage the car finish.

Diesel Fuel Filter

Diesel engines are very susceptible to water in the fuel system. Water will not only cause the engine to sputter or stop, but can actually damage the expensive injection pump or injectors. If you drive a diesel car (or truck), check the owners manual or shop manual for specific information about the diesel fuel system. Most diesel filters have a drain plug which can be used to remove excess water from the bottom of the fuel filter. If the car does not have such a filter, you should install one.

Drain The Fuel Filter

Draining water from the diesel fuel filter is very easy, but can be messy. Be careful not to spill the fuel on any hot engine parts. Drain about one cup of fuel from the bottom of the fuel filter. If water or dirt is found in the fuel, drain another cup of fuel.

Diesel Fuel Contamination

Diesel fuel can become contaminated with a type of fungus. This slimy gooey stuff can clog up the fuel system and cause all types of problems. Keep the tank at least 1/2 full and avoid using old fuel. Special chemicals are available to help remove or prevent the fungus from forming. If the fungus is a continuing problem, flush the fuel tank and fuel system completely, install a new fuel filter, and start buying fuel at a different place.

Drain about one cup of fuel from the bottom of the fuel filter.

Things To Do Every 6 Months

1. Rotate and balance the tires. If balancing is not free, balance the tires once a year.

2. Inspect the brakes: Pad thickness; Drum / Rotor condition; Leaks in system. Repair as needed.

3. Check the wheel bearings. Lubricate or replace as needed.

4. Test the shock absorbers or struts. Replace as needed.

5. Clean the carburetor & choke.

6. Adjust the engine valves (not hydraulic type).

7. Check the manual clutch pedal. Adjust, if necessary.

8. Polish the car.

9. Drain water from the diesel fuel filter (diesels only).

Additional items for your car:

Every Year

The annual check-up for your car is an important part of a total car conservation safety program. Invest in inexpensive and easy to change fluids, filters, and ignition parts before you spend money on expensive computerized tests or complex adjustments. If your car starts easily, runs good, and has normal fuel economy (MPG), it should not need any complex adjustment or major repairs. Car conservation keeps your car in safe driving condition and saves time and money on unnecessary repairs.

Always do the easy and inexpensive maintenance items before paying for the more expensive tests or adjustments.

Air Filter

The engine needs both air and gasoline. In fact, it **needs** much more air than gasoline. For every gallon of gasoline used by the engine, it requires about 10,000 gallons of air.

Before the air goes into the engine it must pass through the air filter. If the air filter becomes clogged, the engine will not run properly or it will waste gasoline (lower MPG). The air filter could break and allow dirty air to enter the engine, causing major damage. Changing the air filter is very easy, the ideal task for a car conservationist.

Types Of Air Filters

If your car has a carburetor, the air filters will be round and located on top of the engine. If your car is fuel injected, the air filter is flat and located off to the side of the engine. Some air filters are made with dark fiber materials which make a visual inspection for dirt very difficult, if not impossible.

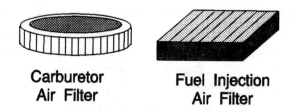

Carburetor Air Filter   **Fuel Injection Air Filter**

Reusable Filters

Reusable air filters are now available for most cars. These foam filters can be removed, washed, and reused for the life of the vehicle. The high initial cost and extra time needed to clean this filter should be considered; however, these filters are good for your car and the environment. If you use this type of filter, be sure to clean it at least once a year.

Replace the air filter each year. A dirty filter can damage the engine, waste fuel, and cause pollution.

Fuel Filter

The fuel filter removes dirt and water from the fuel supply. Dirt or water can cause the engine to sputter or clog up the carburetor or injectors. Some cars have two filters: one for dirt, another for water.

Fuel Pump

A fuel pump is needed to push the gasoline from the fuel tank through the filter and into the engine. If the fuel filter gets clogged up, the pump cannot deliver enough fuel to keep the engine running, especially at higher speeds when the engine needs more fuel.

If the car runs out of fuel or the fuel filter becomes clogged, the fuel pump can overheat and be damaged.

87

Fuel Flow

Fuel filters are marked with an arrow to indicate the proper direction of flow. Install the filter so the arrow points toward the engine.

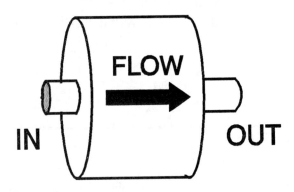

Changing A Fuel Filter

Fuel filters are easy to change, but some are easier than others. A carburetor engine may have the filter(s) located anywhere between the fuel tank and engine. It may be behind the rear wheel (near the fuel tank), near the engine, or inside the carburetor. Look for a red hose, which usually indicates a fuel line. When you find the filter, simply loosen the hose clamps to remove the hose from the old filter. On fuel injected engines, you must eliminate any remaining pressure in the fuel lines before removing the filter. Check the shop manual for specific instructions about changing the fuel filter(s) found on your car.

The fuel filter arrow points towards the engine.

Sparkplugs

Sparkplugs provide the electrical spark needed to ignite the fuel and air mixture inside the engine. If the sparkplug is dirty or burned, the engine may be hard to start or it might sputter. Sparkplugs are the most important ignition item on your car.

Be sure to use the right sparkplug in your car. Sparkplugs come in various shapes and sizes. The owners manual, shop manual, decal underneath the hood, or mechanic can tell you which plug is needed in your car. Of course, you can also remove one of the plugs from the engine and check the type and number.

Heat Range

There are different heat ranges of a sparkplugs: Hot, Regular, and Cold. The regular type of sparkplug is recommended for most driving conditions. WARNING: A hot sparkplug can cause pinging (engine noise) or engine damage.

Special Sparkplugs

Several new types of expensive sparkplugs which claim improved performance and longer life are available. Although these plugs can be expected to last longer, the regular, less expensive plugs are dependable, easy to change, and recommended for most driving conditions. Any sparkplug should last longer in a newer car because of the improved electronic ignition system. All sparkplugs should be removed for inspection and cleaning once a year; therefore, why not install new plugs?

GAP

Gap

The most important part of installing a sparkplug is checking the gap, or distance between the electrodes on the bottom of the plug. A typical gap is 30 thousandths of an inch (.030 inches) or about 1 mm. If the gap is too wide, the spark may be too weak to jump the gap, causing the engine to sputter or loose power. If the gap is too small, it may get clogged up and foul the plug.

Use a round sparkplug tool to measure the gap, not a flat feeler gauge. If the gap distance is given as a range, adjust the gap closer to the lower (smaller) setting because the gap tends to widen with use. Do not press against the center electrode when adjusting the gap; this can damage the sparkplug. Bend the outer tab (electrode) carefully to adjust the gap.

Other Sparkplug Tips

Remove the sparkplugs when the engine is cold. Grasp the rubber boot, not the wire itself, to remove the sparkplug wire. Clean around each sparkplug so no dirt or water will fall into the engine. Change one plug at a time to avoid mixing up the sparkplug wires. Use a little anti-seize compound on the threads of each new plug. Start each sparkplug by hand, to avoid cross threading, and then tighten them securely using a sparkplug tool. Do not overtighten the sparkplugs, which can cause damage.

Measure and adjust the gap on each sparkplug before installation.

Distributor Cap & Rotor

The distributor cap and rotor sends the electrical spark to the proper sparkplug at the right time. Although most newer cars have computerized electronic ignitions systems, many still have a distributor cap and rotor. The distributor cap is the plastic top of the distributor. The rotor is the small arm underneath the cap, which turns when the engine is running. NOTE: *Rotor* is also a term used for the brake disc.

The distributor cap and rotor wear out and become corroded due to the electrical currents. After some time they become burnt or corroded and cannot transmit the spark very well, causing a weak spark (or no spark) to arrive at the sparkplug. This can cause a rough idle and waste fuel. If the distributor cap or rotor is cracked or damaged, the engine may not start or run at all. Installing a new cap and rotor will help ensure that a good spark is arriving at each sparkplug.

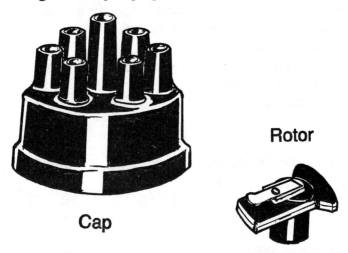

Rotor

Cap

Replace The Cap & Rotor

The cap and rotor are easy to remove with only a screwdriver or pliers. Move one wire at a time from the old cap to the new cap. This ensures that each wire fits into the proper hole. Apply a small amount of dielectric grease to the metal end of each sparkplug wire to assure a good connection. If the sparkplug wires cannot be removed from the cap (one piece assembly), replace these parts every two years.

Replace the distributor cap and rotor. Install each sparkplug wire into the proper hole on the distributor cap.

PCV Valve

The Positive Crankcase Ventilation (PCV) valve has been used on most engines for over 30 years. This little valve removes contaminated air from inside the engine, which increases fuel economy, reduces pollution, and extends the life of the engine.

The PCV valve is usually located near the top of the engine between the valve cover and air filter. Many PCV valves are inserted into a rubber hose and do not require any tools to remove. There may also be a small filter associated with the PCV system, sometimes called the blow-by filter. If so, replace this filter, too.

Replace The PCV Valve

Replace both the PCV valve and filter each year to be sure the system operates properly. If the PCV valve becomes clogged, the engine may start to leak oil, pollute the air, or not pass the exhaust gas emission tests.

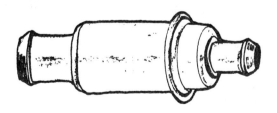

A clogged PCV valve can cause the engine to leak oil and pollute the air.

Engine Timing

Engine timing refers to getting the electrical sparks to the right sparkplug at the right time so the fuel and air mixture can burn properly inside the engine. If it arrives too early or too late (or not at all), the engine lacks power, wastes fuel, and may sputter or stop. The timing is set while the engine is at idle speed; however, the engine must adjust the timing automatically when it turns faster.

Ignition systems have been greatly improved during the past 15 years. Newer engines utilize electronic ignition, which requires less maintenance and fewer adjustments. However, proper timing is still critical to efficient engine operation. Some cars have complete computer controlled systems and no adjustments are necessary or possible. Many cars, however, require timing adjustments. Use a timing light to check when the spark is arriving at the #1 sparkplug. Loosen the distributor and rotate it slowly to the right or left to adjust the timing in accordance with the instructions in the shop manual.

NOTE: Very few cars on the road today are equipped with points and condensers as part of the ignition system. However, if your car has these parts, replace them before testing or adjusting the timing.

Test It Yourself

Testing the engine timing is very easy. Even if you do not have the tools or training to adjust the timing, you can still use a timing light to test the engine and then take the car to a mechanic if it requires adjustments.

Check the timing to be sure the sparkplugs are getting the sparks at the right time.

Tune-Up

What is a tune-up? Almost every mechanic has their own definition of a tune-up. This is why the price can range from a few dollars to several hundred dollars. The tune-up should involve minor adjustments of the engine so it will start easily, run properly, and achieve normal fuel economy. The tune-up should not include major repairs; however, you will not know what to expect unless you ask, "What exactly are you going to do and how much is charged for parts and labor?"

Cheap Tune-Ups

Most inexpensive tune-ups consist of several quick inspections and installing new sparkplugs. You pay $50 for four sparkplugs ($5 parts + $20 labor + $25 profit). That's all you really get; unfortunately, it may not be enough. Other items, such as the air filter, fuel filter, distributor cap, rotor, or PCV valve may need to be replaced, too. Of course, these extra items are not included in the basic price. This is why the inexpensive tune-up can end up costing you over a hundred dollars.

All tune-ups are not the same. Find out what parts are actually being replaced on your car.

Idle Speed

After the minor parts (sparkplugs, filters, cap, rotor, PCV valve, etc.) are replaced and the engine timing has been adjusted, the idle speed should be checked. A fast idle wastes fuel, causes excess pollution, and can be dangerous. A slow idle may cause the engine to cut off every time you slow down. Most newer cars with computer controls do not need frequent adjustments; however, if the idle speed is not within shop manual specifications, make the necessary adjustments. These adjustments are usually very easy to do. If your car has a tachometer, use it to determine if the idle speed, which is listed on the decal under the hood, is within the correct range.

Transmission Fluid

The transmission delivers power from the engine to the wheels. Your car might have either a manual or automatic transmission. The manual transmission will deliver slightly higher fuel economy (MPG), however, with improved designs in automatic transmissions, the difference is small, especially at highway speeds. Rear wheel drive cars have a separate differential gear located between the rear wheels. Four wheel drive (4WD) cars have two differential gears and a separate part of the transmission called the transfer case.

Change the automatic transmission fluid, manual transmission oil, differential oil, and transfer case oil each year.

Lifetime Fluids

Some cars have been driven for years without changing these fluids and newer transmission fluids claim to be good for the life of the car. However, many of these cars experienced expensive transmission problems. Changing these fluids is easy and much less expensive than any repair. If you want your car to be dependable and last a long time, become a car conservationist.

Automatic Transmission

The automatic transmission uses a special fluid, or oil, called Automatic Transmission Fluid (ATF). This fluid operates both the transmission and clutch. On most transmissions, it is impossible to drain out all the old fluid. Therefore, it is a good idea to change this fluid each year. You can do this yourself, but most transmission shops will change the fluid and replace the filter for about $40.

If the transmission has a replaceable filter, install a new one. If the transmission has a permanent metal filter, wash it thoroughly in clean automatic transmission fluid and reinstall it. Use a new gasket on the transmission pan and tighten it evenly to prevent leaks.

Dexron or Type F

There are several types of ATF available today: Dexron and Type F are two of the most common. Check the owners manual and use the recommended type of fluid. Do not mix different types of fluid or overfill the transmission. New synthetic transmission fluid may not be recommended nor needed for your car.

Manual Transmission

The manual transmission uses oil to lubricate the gears and permit smooth shifting of the transmission. Check the oil level by removing the fill plug on the side of the transmission. The oil level should be at the bottom of the fill hole. Drain the oil by removing the drain plug at the bottom of the transmission. Replace the drain plug (install a new gasket) and refill to the bottom of the fill hole with the type of oil specified in the owners manual. The manual transmission will normally use a very thick oil, such as SAE 90. However, sometimes SAE 30 engine oil or ATF is recommended. The manual transmission does not have a filter.

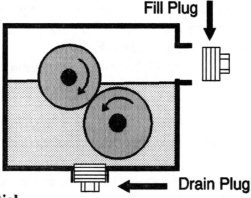

Differential

The differential on a front wheel drive car is part of the transmission (called the trans-axle). The differential on a rear wheel drive car is located between the rear wheels. Another differential will be found between the front wheels of a four wheel (all wheel) drive car. The differential receives power from the transmission and delivers it to the wheels. It also allows the wheels to turn at slightly different speeds as the car turns a corner.

The differential has a drain and fill plug, similar to the manual transmission. Use the type of oil recommended in the owners manual or shop manual. A special thick oil, such as SAE 90, is usually required. The differential does not have a filter.

Transfer Case

A four wheel drive car may have a separate part of the transmission called the transfer case. It allows power to be directed toward two wheels, all four wheels, or no wheels (neutral). The transfer case will also have a drain and fill plug, similar to the manual transmission. Use the type of oil recommended in the owners manual or shop manual. A thick oil, such as SAE 90, is usually required. The transfer case does not have a filter.

Changing the transmission fluid or oil is very easy and helps prevent leaks in the transmission and keeps the transmission shifting smoothly.

Exhaust & Pollution Systems

Every year the car should have a complete inspection of the exhaust system and pollution controls. Broken pipes, loose vacuum hoses, or electrical malfunctions can cause the car to run poorly or pollute the air. Many muffler shops will perform free inspections. Fortunately, with the new unleaded fuels available today, the exhaust and pollution control systems should last more than five years before needing to be replaced.

Carbon Monoxide

One of the most dangerous exhaust gases is carbon monoxide. This colorless, odorless, and tasteless gas is produced when there is not enough oxygen mixed with the fuel. If the exhaust system is broken or clogged, or if the car is sitting still with the engine running, carbon monoxide can get into the passenger compartment and cause headaches, dizziness, nausea, or sickness. Without adequate ventilation, you may pass out and die. If you feel sick while driving, roll down a window and get some fresh air. Never stay inside a parked car while the engine is running if the windows are closed and never run the engine when the car is inside a closed garage.

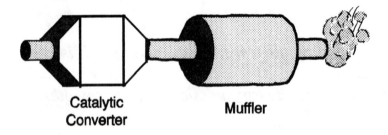

Catalytic Converter   **Muffler**

Oxygenated Fuels

Some cities use oxygenated fuel (during winter) to reduce the amount of carbon monoxide in the exhaust gases. The oil companies have several methods of adding oxygen to the fuel: ethanol, methanal, or ether products. Two types of alcohol are commonly used as additives. Ethanol is a renewable resource. Methanol may cause damage to the fuel system or engine and health problems. Consult the owners manual or your mechanic for recommendations about which fuel is best for your car.

Emission Warranty

All cars come with a special warranty on the emission control systems of five years or 50,000 miles. With the exception of the PCV valve, these systems should outlast the warranty without any maintenance or adjustments. The CHECK ENGINE warning light may indicate a problem with a emission control system or just remind you to have the systems inspected. Many newer cars use the CHECK ENGINE light to indicate the trouble codes from the engine computer. Refer to the owners manual or shop manual for more information about the warning lights.

E.G.R. Valve

The Exhaust Gas Recirculation (EGR) valve allows some exhaust gases to be blended with the fuel-air mixture in order to reduce pollution. This valve requires no periodic maintenance or adjustments, but should be replaced every five years or 75,000 miles. If it malfunctions the car will run poorly and may not pass the emissions test. Refer to the shop manual for more information.

O_2 Sensor

The O_2 (oxygen) sensor is attached to the exhaust pipe to monitor the amount of unburned oxygen in the exhaust gases. The sensor sends a signal to the engine computer to adjust the fuel-air mixture for optimal performance and efficiency. This sensor requires no periodic maintenance or adjustment, but should be replaced every five years or 75,000 miles. If it malfunctions, the car will run poorly and may not pass the emissions test. Refer to the shop manual for more information.

A.I.R. Pump

The Air Injection Reaction (AIR) pump injects air into the carburetor, exhaust manifold, or catalytic converter to reduce harmful pollution. This pump is turned by a belt on the engine. If the pump breaks, the belt may begin to squeal and then suddenly break or the pump may start to make strange noises.

The AIR pump requires no maintenance or adjustments, but may need to be replaced every five years or 75,000 miles. If the AIR pump is replaced, install a new check valve and test the diverter valve for proper operation. Refer to the shop manual for more information.

Charcoal Canister

The charcoal canister is another part of the emission control system. It absorbs and stores excess fuel vapors to prevent air pollution. The canister does not need any periodic maintenance or adjustments, but should be replaced every five years or 75,000 miles.

The charcoal canister can be damaged if the fuel tank is overfilled. A damaged canister can cause the car to fail the emissions test. Testing and replacing the charcoal canister is easy in most cars. Refer to the shop manual for more information.

Have the exhaust system and pollution controls tested each year.

Annual Safety Inspection

Most states require an annual safety inspection. Some inspections are quick and easy, others require more scrutiny and testing. The goal of this test is to be sure all cars are road worthy and safe. This goal, unfortunately, is not always achieved.

Before The Inspection

There are several easy things you can do to be sure your car will pass this inspection easily. Check the lights and turn signals for proper operation. If the bulb is not working, check the fuse box for a broken fuse. If the bulb is burned out, replace it. Check the wipers. If they are old or brittle, replace them. Check the horn.

If the car must undergo the exhaust emissions test, replace the engine oil, oil filter, air filter, fuel filter, sparkplugs, cap & rotor, and PCV valve & filter. These inexpensive and easy to replace parts can greatly affect the efficiency and performance of the engine. Drive the car for about 30 minutes at highway speeds to warm up the engine and emission controls before taking the emissions test.

Drive your car at highway speeds for about 30 minutes to warm up the engine and exhaust system before taking the emissions test.

Things To Do Every Year

1. Replace air filter.

2. Replace fuel filter.

3. Replace sparkplugs.

4. Replace distributor cap & rotor.

5. Replace PCV valve.

6. Check engine timing.

7. Tune-up procedure.

8. Replace transmission fluids:
   * Automatic transmission fluid & filter
   * Manual transmission oil
   * Differential oil (RWD)
   * Transfer case oil (4WD)

9. Test exhaust gases.

10. Preform annual safety inspection.

Additional items for your car:

Every Two Years

Every other year the car needs some additional maintenance on several important parts to provide an extra measure of safety and reliability. Of course, it is easy to keep postponing needed maintenance until something breaks and must be repaired immediately; however, you will save time and money if you practice good car conservation. One of the biggest benefits of car conservation is flexibility and convenience. Instead of your car breaking down on the side of the road, you can shop for the best price on parts and schedule the service at a time convenient both for you and the mechanic. You also get to choose a good mechanic, not the nearest one. Keep your car running safely for many years with smart car conservation.

Car conservation helps you drive with confidence.

Wipers

Windshield wipers are an important safety feature on your car. Unfortunately, you might think about them only when it starts to rain. Dirty or old wipers will clatter or cause streaks on the windows. This can distract you or limit your visibility.

Check the wipers when you wash the car. Look for cracks or other damage to the rubber pieces. Clean the wipers with a rubber protectant to help keep them soft and flexible.

Blades & Inserts

A wiper blade refers to the metal and rubber portion of the wiper. Blades are usually easier to install, but they are more expensive. The insert is just the rubber portion of the wiper. If you have the choice, buy inserts for your car.

Wiper Blade

Installing New Wipers

Replace the wipers every two years, or when they become damaged. Wipers are inexpensive and easy to install, usually without tools (or only a small screwdriver). Instructions are provided with the replacement wipers or you can ask your mechanic for help. Wipers often come with a variety of adapters and you will need to attach the ones for your car.

Wipers are inexpensive and easy to install, usually without any tools.

Brake Fluid

Brake fluid is a light brown liquid specially design to operate at the very high temperatures in the brake system. Dirt or water mixed with brake fluid will cause it to turn dark and damage the rubber seals, causing leaks in the brake system. Once the rubber seals are damaged and begin to leak, the car may not stop safely and the more expensive parts of the system, such as master cylinder and calipers, must be replaced.

Use the type of brake fluid recommended in the owners manual. Silicon (or permanent) brake fluid may damage some brake systems.

Change The Brake Fluid

Changing the brake fluid every two years will prevent damage to the rubber seals, save time and money in brake repairs, and avoid spilling this dangerous fluid into the environment. If your car has a manual clutch operated with brake fluid, change it, too.

Cars with anti-lock brake systems, or ABS, may require changing the brake fluid more often (annually or semi-annually).

Manual Bleed Method

Changing the brake fluid is easy, but you must prevent air bubbles from getting into the brake system. There is a bleed screw located at each wheel. Start at the wheel farthest from the brake pedal or master cylinder. Install a clear hose on the bleed screw and put the other end in a small container. Then have someone push (and hold) the brake pedal. Open the bleed screw to force the old fluid out (the pedal should sink to the floor). Then close the bleed screw. And finally, release the pedal to draw in fresh brake fluid from the reservoir.

Add more clean fluid to the reservoir, as needed to maintain at least a 1/2 FULL level. Repeat these steps until the fluid coming out of the bleed screw is clean and without bubbles. Do this at each wheel until all the old fluid has been flushed from the system. Finally, fill the reservoir to the FULL level and fasten the cap securely. Take the old brake fluid to a recycling center for disposal. Check the shop manual for the exact location of the bleed screws and specific instructions for your car..

Open ; Pedal Down ; Close ; Pedal Up.

Power Bleed Method

The mechanic may use a power bleed method to change the brake fluid. This method is much faster and can be done by one person. It requires about 30 minutes labor and 1/2 gallon of brake fluid for the average car.

Test drive the car at slow speeds in a safe area after any brake repair.

Power Steering Fluid

Power steering fluid can also get dirty and collect moisture from the air. This can damage the power steering pump or cause leaks in the system. Change the power steering fluid to prevent leaks or damage to the more expensive steering parts.

Change The P/S Fluid

Disconnect the upper hose (return line) from the side of the power steering fluid reservoir. Put the end of this hose in a suitable container away from moving or hot engine parts. Cover the opening on the reservoir to prevent any fluid from leaking out. Start the engine for about 5 seconds to pump the old fluid into the container.

Turn the engine OFF and reconnect the hose to the P/S reservoir. Fill the reservoir to the FULL level with fresh power steering fluid. Start the engine for a few seconds, then turn the engine OFF. Refill to the FULL level, if necessary. Then drive the car slowly, turning the steering wheel full left and full right several times to remove any air bubbles from the system. Turn the engine OFF and check the fluid level again. Refill to the FULL level, if necessary. Take the old power steering fluid to a recycling center for disposal. Refer to the shop manual for specific instructions about changing the P/S fluid in your car.

Use the type of P/S fluid recommended in the owners manual or shop manual. The wrong type of fluid can damage the P/S system.

Radiator Fluid

Radiator fluid circulates through the engine and radiator to maintain a constant temperature. The engine runs best and produces the least amount of pollution when it operates at the normal engine temperature. A cold engine runs poorly and wastes fuel and a very hot engine will overheat and be ruined.

The radiator fluid is a mixture of water and coolant (or anti-freeze). All cars should use coolant to prevent rust, lubricate the water pump, and keep the engine from overheating during hot weather or freezing in very cold weather.

50:50 Mixture

Most cars need a 50:50 mixture of coolant and water. Only in very cold climates, like northern Canada, should you need a stronger 70% coolant and 30% water mixture. Do not use pure coolant as radiator fluid; it will cause the engine to overheat.

Change The Radiator Fluid

If the radiator fluid is over two years old, change it. Flush the system with a radiator cleaner, only if the old radiator fluid is brown or very dirty. If the radiator fluid is one year old, buy a can of rust inhibitor and water pump lubricant at the auto store and add it to the expansion tank. Change the fluid next year (every two years).

Lifetime Coolant

Some coolant is made to last four years or 60,000 miles. It should last longer because it costs more! However, the rust inhibitors and water pump lubricants may not last that long. Car conservation means cost effective car care, not spending more and getting less. Keep the engine cooling system in great shape with biennial fluid changes.

Avoid "Drain-n-Fill" radiator specials. You need to change the fluid in the entire radiator system, not just the fluid in the radiator.

Eco-Antifreeze

A new antifreeze is available which is made from a different chemical (propylene glycol) and is less poisonous than regular coolant (ethylene glycol). It costs more and offers lower performance! It contains safer chemicals, but it is still poisonous. Do not mix this coolant with regular coolant; it will be impossible to accurately test a mixture. A true car conservationist always uses caution with any car fluid, fixes leaks, recycles when possible, and disposes of old fluids properly.

Reuse Old Radiator Fluid

Some repair shops have special equipment which can recycle the old radiator fluid. This machine removes the old fluid from your car, filters its, adjusts the Ph, adds new rust inhibitors and water pump lubricants, modifies the concentration, and then reinstalls the clean fluid. It is a great way to be a car conservationist and recycle!

Do It Yourself

If you want to change the radiator fluid yourself, purchase a radiator flushing kit at the auto store. The plastic "T" can be installed in one of the heater hoses to greatly simplify the procedure. Turn the heater selector to HOT and use a garden hose to flush out the old fluid. Then add about one gallon of coolant to the system and replace the caps. Save the old radiator fluid and send it to a recycling center.

Radiator fluid is poisonous, but has a sweet taste. Use caution around children and small animals. Recycle the old radiator fluid.

Air Conditioning

The air conditioning system is one item which does require special training and tools to test and repair. The high pressure gas is dangerous and special precautions are required by law to avoid damage to the environment. Therefore, it is a good idea to let a qualified automotive technician service this system every two years. If the air conditioner leaks, fix the leak before adding more gas; otherwise, the gas may quickly leak out, wasting money, causing pollution, and damaging the expensive compressor.

Refrigerant

The air conditioning system operates on a supply of gas, or refrigerant, and like the other systems we have discussed, there is a maximum and minimum range. It is important to maintain the supply of refrigerant between these two limits. The maximum amount of gas allows for proper safe operation; however, any more gas may cause the seals to leak or hoses to burst. The minimum amount of gas also permits safe operation, but, any less gas can damage the compressor or not allow adequate cooling effect. Most cars are now equipped with a switch which senses very low pressure in the A/C system and will not allow the compressor to operate, thus preventing damage.

Older cars are equipped with R-12 refrigerant. Newer cars use R-134a. These refrigerants are not compatible and neither are the A/C parts or test equipment. Therefore, all A/C system repairs should be done by a qualified and licensed A/C technician.

Prevent Leaks

Recycle Refrigerants

New equipment provides a method of removing the old gas, filtering out dirt, oil, water, and then replacing the clean gas. Additional gas is added, as needed. This is a good way to recycle and reuse the refrigerant and save some money on A/C repairs.

Any leak in the air conditioning system should be fixed to avoid serious damage to the expensive compressor or the environment.

Wheel Alignment

The exact position of each wheel is very important for safe handling of the car and long tire life. Most cars with rear wheel drive only need the front wheels aligned. Front wheel drive cars usually need all four wheels aligned. Proper wheel alignment will help make the tires wear evenly and last longer. This saves money and reduces the amount of used tires in our landfills.

Wheel Adjustments

The front wheels are the hardest to adjust because they move from side to side when the car is turning. There are several adjustments, such as caster, camber, toe-in, and toe-out, all of which must be double checked when any one adjustment is made. The adjustments are very small and must be made with quality precision equipment and by a properly trained patient technician.

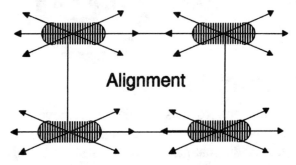

Aligning the wheels every two years is a good general recommendation. There are other times, however, when it makes sense to have the wheels aligned: when purchasing new tires, replacing the struts, following any accident, after hitting a hard bump, when the car pulls to one side, or when you notice unusual tire wear.

Lifetime Wheel Alignment

Some repair shops offer a lifetime (or multi-year) alignment program, which can be a great deal if your car is not too old and you plan to keep it a long time. Because wheel alignment is only an adjustment (some cars require some small shims), try to negotiate a free or reduced price alignment when you purchase new struts or tires.

Wheel alignment usually requires no parts. It does require precision testing equipment and a patient technician with adequate training and experience.

Fuel Injection

When fuel injected engines were first introduced, the gasoline available was not designed for these engines and the injectors were not very good quality. Therefore, some injectors got clogged quickly and the engines would not perform properly. Today, however, fuel injection is very common and the gasoline has been specially modified with additives to prevent clogging and keep the injectors clean. Improvements in fuel injector design have also been implemented.

Regular - Plus - Premium

When comparing the different types of fuel, such as regular, plus, or premium, the only major difference is the octane rating (resistance to ping). All grades of fuel contain similar cleaning additives. Although different

115

companies do use different cleaning additives, they all do an excellent job at keeping both carburetors and injectors clean. Do not be misled by advertisements which imply that your car should start easier, run better, or last longer when using the more expensive fuels.

Premium Fuel

Premium fuel (higher octane) does not clean better or provide extra power. It will, however, resist engine knock or ping. If the engine in your car pings, first change the sparkplugs (if they are over one year old) and adjust the engine timing. If it still pings, you may need the Plus or Premium type fuel. An car with more than 100,000 miles or some high performance cars may need higher octane fuel to prevent pinging.

Knock Sensors

Some fuel injected cars have a knock sensor which prevents engine knock, and you might notice that the car runs slightly better with higher octane fuel. The best fuel recommendation will be found in the owners manual. If it says use 87 Octane fuel, use it. Measure the gas mileage. Then try some higher octane fuel and measure the mileage again. You cannot damage the engine by using higher octane fuel, but you can waste money.

Most cars are designed to run on 87 octane or regular fuel. Using more expensive fuel in this type of car is a waste of money and will not provide more performance, a cleaner engine, better fuel economy, or lower emissions.

Cleaning Fuel Injectors

There are several methods of cleaning fuel injectors. The easiest and least effective method is to pour a can of cleaner into the fuel tank before filling up. You can buy a can of fuel injector cleaner at the auto store and do this yourself. A better and more expensive method is to pump a special cleaner through the system under high pressure. The best method and most expensive method is to remove the injectors and disassemble, clean, and test each one. Another choice is to simply replace the injectors with new ones.

Check the fuel economy (MPG). As long as the MPG remains within a normal range, the injectors should not need cleaning.

Things To Do Every 2 Years

1. Replace the wipers.

2. Replace the brake fluid.

3. Replace the power steering fluid.

4. Service the air conditioning system.

5. Check the wheel alignment.
   Castor; Chamber; Toe-In; Toe-Out.
   Do this when installing struts or buying new tires.

6. Clean the fuel injectors (if necessary).

Additional items for your car:

Every Four Years

Four years is a critical time in the life of your car. You have several choices. First, you can trade the car in for a newer model which does not need as much maintenance. Newer cars, however, are very expensive and the monthly car payments keep the cost-per-mile very high. Secondly, you can keep driving the car and hope nothing breaks. However, when something does break, a major repair can be very costly and inconvenient.

The best way to keep the car running safely and reliably for many years is with preventive maintenance. Car conservation saves time, money, and reduces the cost-per-mile. It keeps older cars in safe, reliable condition and out of the junk yards. Recycle your car with preventive maintenance.

Car conservation saves time, money, and reduces the cost-per-mile.

Battery

The battery provides the power needed to start the car. If the battery lacks power or if the power in the battery cannot get to the starter motor, the engine will not start. Check the battery connections, as mentioned in Chapter 4, before recharging or replacing the battery. A good time to buy a battery is in late summer or early fall, before the cold weather arrives.

Cold Weather

When it is cold, the battery must work extra hard. The chemical reaction inside the battery slows down, and therefore the battery has less power in cold weather. If the battery is not fully charged, it can freeze. The engine oil becomes thicker in cold weather and makes cranking the engine much harder. Cold fuel does not vaporize or burn easily, which also makes starting a cold engine more difficult. These are three main reasons why most battery problems occur during cold weather.

Check the battery in your car before cold weather arrives.

Cold Cranking Amps

The battery is rated in Cold Cranking Amps (CCA). This is a measure of the power available in the battery when it is at 0°F or -18°C. Higher CCA represents more power, which means the battery should last longer and have more reserve power. When you purchase a new battery, buy one with the same or slightly greater CCA than the old battery. Be sure the battery and terminals fit safely in the battery compartment in the car.

The correct CCA value represents the power available at 0°F or -18°C.

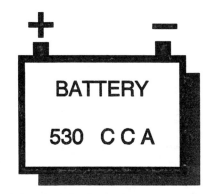

530 Cold Cranking Amps
@ 0 degrees F

Very Expensive Batteries

Some batteries are rated for 72 months or six years of service or come with extra reserve power. When you consider the very high initial cost of these batteries, the probability that it will die during the sixth year, and the dangers involved with a breakdown or jumpstart, these batteries may not be such a great deal. The very expensive batteries may have a longer warranty, but, read the fine print to determine any real benefits. You can save time and money by replacing the battery every four years and avoiding the very expensive batteries.

Recycle Batteries

Car batteries should be recycled. Most auto stores require a trade-in battery or deposit when you purchase a new battery. Return any old batteries to the auto store or recycling center for recycling or proper disposal. The acid and lead in old batteries is dangerous to people and the environment.

Batteries are very heavy. Recycle the old battery.

Radiator Cap

The radiator cap regulates the pressure in the radiator system. As the engine warms up, the radiator fluid expands. The radiator cap allows some of the hot radiator fluid to drain out of the radiator and into the expansion tank reservoir. Then, as the engine cools down, the cap allows some fluid to be syphoned back into the radiator. This enables the radiator to remain completely full at all times and helps prevent rust inside the cooling system.

Replace The Cap

The rubber gasket or metal spring in the radiator cap can weaken or break after many years of use. A damaged cap can allow the radiator fluid to leak out or cause the engine to overheat. Radiator caps are not expensive or difficult to install. Replace the cap every four years.

Removing The Radiator Cap

Remove the radiator cap when the engine is cold. Cover the cap with a rag and press down while turning the cap slowly to the left (counter clockwise). To install a new cap, press down and turn the cap all the way to the right (clock wise).

Do not remove a hot radiator cap; very hot steam can burn you. Install a new radiator cap when the engine is cold.

Radiator Hoses

Radiator hoses are the rubber hoses which allow the hot radiator fluid to circulate between the engine and radiator(s). If a radiator hose breaks, the radiator fluid will leak out and the engine will overheat.

Hoses

There are four radiator hoses on all cars. Two large hoses connect the engine to the radiator at the front of the car. Two smaller hoses connect the heater system to the engine. Many cars have other hoses near the thermostat or engine. Refer to the shop manual for the exact location of all radiator hoses on your car.

Check the radiator hoses every two months, as discussed in Chapter 4. Any small leak or unusual damage should be repaired immediately. However, when the hoses are four years old, they should be changed. Even hoses which look normal may be deteriorating on the inside after many years of use.

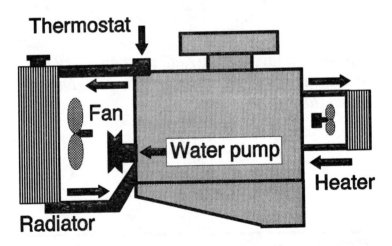

The lower radiator hose is usually attached to the water pump. This hose is often stiffer and may have a wire coil insert to prevent it from collapsing from the suction of the pump. Good quality hoses made for your car are available at a reasonable price from local auto stores.

Hose Clamps

Hose clamps are attached to each end of the radiator hoses. These clamps prevent leaks and hold the hoses in place. Always use new clamps when installing a new hose. Do not overtighten the clamps, which can cut or damage the hose.

Install new clamps with every new hose. Do not overtighten the clamps.

Thermostat

The thermostat is a temperature controlled valve. It regulates the flow of radiator fluid to control the engine temperature. When the engine is cold, the thermostat closes and forces the radiator fluid to circulate inside the engine. This causes the engine to warm up quickly. As the engine warms up, the thermostat opens to allow the fluid to circulate through the radiator, as needed, to maintain the proper temperature.

Cold & Hot

Both a cold and very hot engine are harmful. Cold engines waste fuel, cause excess pollution, and will not run very well. Very hot engines can overheat and cause serious engine damage. The proper engine temperature allows smooth operation, normal fuel economy, minimum engine wear, and lower levels of pollution.

Normal Operating Temperature

The engine should achieve normal operating temperature in five to ten minutes. If the thermostat is stuck in the open position, the engine will take much longer to warm up. If the thermostat is stuck closed, the engine will overheat. Notice the normal position of the indicator on the temperature gauge in your car and the time it takes to reach this position.

Thermostat

The thermostat is usually located where the upper large radiator hose is attached to the engine. Several small bolts hold the cover, or housing, in place. Drain the fluid from the radiator before replacing the thermostat. Install the new gasket which comes with the thermostat to prevent radiator fluid leaks. Change the thermostat when you install new radiator hoses. Refer to the shop manual for specific instructions.

Do not drive the car when the thermostat is removed or not working properly; this can cause the engine to overheat.

Water Pump

The water pump circulates the radiator fluid when the engine is running. It is turned by a rubber belt. When the engine is cold, the pump circulates the fluid inside the engine to allow the engine to warm up quickly. As the engine warms up to the normal operating temperature, the thermostat opens to allow the fluid to circulate between the engine and radiator, as needed, to maintain the proper engine temperature.

Warning Signs

Two conditions will quickly damage the water pump (and engine). A low supply of radiator fluid will cause the water pump to overheat. Rust, dirt, or lack of lubricants in the radiator fluid can also damage the water pump. Good maintenance of the radiator fluid, hoses, and thermostat will help keep the water pump operating properly. A damaged water pump will make noise and start leaking.

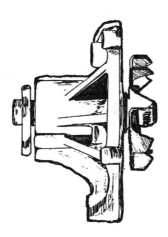

Replace The Water Pump

The water pump bolts onto the front (or side) of the engine. Drain the radiator fluid from the radiator and engine before replacing the water pump. Install a new gasket with the water pump. If the radiator fan is attached to the pump, check it and the fan clutch for damage and replace these items, if necessary. For more specific information, refer to the shop manual.

On many cars, the water pump must be removed to replace the timing belt. Replace both of these items at the same time to save labor cost.

Belts

Flexible rubber belts are used to transmit power from the engine to other rotating items, such as the alternator, water pump, air conditioner compressor, power steering pump, AIR pump, etc. The engine can either have one long belt which operates all the items, or several belts, depending on the options installed on your car.

In Chapter 4 we discussed how to inspect and adjust the tension of the belts every two months. All belts should last four years; however, they should be replaced before they break and damage the engine. You can save money and time by changing all the belts at one time.

Timing Belt

Your car may have a special rubber belt inside the engine, called the timing belt. The timing belt controls the engine valves and is the hardest belt to change. The water pump and other engine belts are usually removed to change the timing belt, therefore most mechanics will suggest replacing all these items at the same time to save on labor cost. NOTE: Some cars have a metal timing chain, which does not need to be replaced, but may need annual adjustments.

Changing A Belt

The hardest part of this job can be getting to the belt or adjustment brackets. Good quality belts are available at your local auto store at reasonable prices. Avoid the adjustable emergency belts which can be cut to fit any size. These belts are hard to install and may cause other damage. Refer to Chapter 4 or the shop manual for specific information about removing a belt or adjusting the tension.

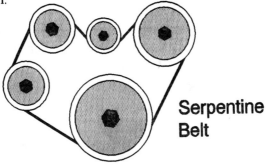

Serpentine
Belt

Replace the engine belts, timing belt, and water pump at the same time to save on labor cost.

Brake Hoses

Brake lines are mostly small metal tubes, that hold the brake fluid. However, near each wheel there is a short section of flexible rubber hose. The rubber brake hoses are needed to provide adequate flexibility to the system. These rubber brake hoses should be inspected every six months, as discussed in Chapter 5, and any damaged hoses should be fixed immediately.

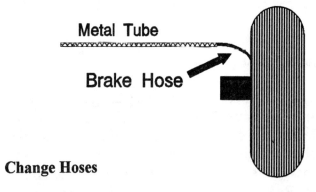

Metal Tube

Brake Hose

Change Hoses

The rubber brake hoses operate under difficult conditions. They are constantly exposed to dirt, water, and road debris. The brake fluid near each wheel also gets very hot during normal use. A leak in one of these brake hoses can cause a collision. Every four years, change these hoses. Use caution to avoid damage to the metal connectors or brake tubes. A good time to replace the brake hoses is when you schedule a brake fluid change, because the brake lines must be bled to remove air from the lines. Refer to Chapter 7 for more information about bleeding the brakes.

Bleed the brake system to remove any air bubbles after changing the brake hoses.

Fuel Cap

The fuel cap does much more than prevent the gasoline from spilling out of the tank. It keeps the vapors inside the tank to reduce air pollution. The fuel cap also allows air to enter the tank as fuel is pumped to the engine. Otherwise, the engine would stop. Never drive without the fuel cap in place. Install a new fuel cap every four years. Fuel caps are inexpensive and available at most auto stores.

Emission Controls

The fuel cap is part of the emission control system on your car. When you remove the fuel cap to fill up the tank, it is normal for there to be a gush of air from the tank. This indicates that the cap and emission system are working properly. Remove the cap slowly and always replace it securely.

Filling Up

Do not overfill the fuel tank. The rubber hose between the fill spout and the fuel tank is not designed to hold fuel. Overfilling can cause a leak or damage the charcoal canister near the engine. On the other hand, do not run out of fuel. Maintain the fuel gauge between 1/2 and FULL. An empty tank is also more likely to collect moisture from the air and cause water or rust inside the tank. Running out of fuel can also damage the expensive fuel pump.

A broken fuel cap can cause the engine to run poorly, waste fuel, and pollute the air.

Fuel Pump

A fuel pump is needed to transfer the gasoline from the tank to the engine. A mechanical fuel pump is bolted onto the side of the engine; however, most cars today (both carburetor and fuel injected engines) use a small electric pump inside the fuel tank.

Test The Fuel Pump

If the car is over four years old, test the fuel pump. If the engine has a carburetor, test both the pressure and volume output of the pump. The fuel pump normally operates at 4 PSI and delivers about 1 quart of fuel every minute. On fuel injected engines, however, the fuel pump produces a much higher pressure of about 40 PSI. Diesel engines produce a much higher pressure. Refer to the shop manual for safe test procedures for the type of pumps in your car. A fuel pump which does not meet the minimum shop manual specifications should be replaced.

Replace The Fuel Pump

If the fuel pump is over six years old, skip the test and simply replace the pump. It may still be within shop specifications, but it will not last forever. The mechanical type pumps, which are bolted onto the side of the engine, are the easiest to replace. An electric fuel pump inside the fuel tank can usually be removed from an access hole inside the trunk. Replacing the fuel pump on a diesel engine requires special training and tools and is the most expensive. Refer to the shop manual for more information.

If the fuel pump is four years old, have it tested.
If it is over six years old, replace it.

Sparkplug Wires

Sparkplug wires transmit the spark from the distributor cap to the sparkplugs. If these wires are damaged or broken, the engine may sputter or not run at all. Unfortunately, damage to these wires occurs on the inside and, therefore visual inspections are not adequate.

Test The Wires

It is possible to remove each wire and test it using a Volt-Ohm-Meter (VOM). However, this test is not always accurate, or it simply tells you what you already know: the wires are old and need to be replaced. It is much easier and cost effective to install new sparkplug wires every four years.

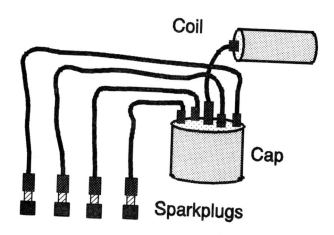

Install A Set

Sparkplug wires come in complete sets, including the wire from the distributor to the ignition coil. Replace the wires one at a time to be sure each sparkplug is attached to the proper hole on the distributor. Hold the rubber boot at the end of the wires; never pull on the wire itself. Good quality wires for most cars can be purchased at the local auto store at a considerable savings over official dealership parts. Avoid buying a set of cheap wires; they may not last very long or provide good performance. Apply a little di-electric grease to each terminal to ensure a good contact between the wire and sparkplug.

Replace the sparkplug wires one at a time to be sure each is connected to the proper hole in the distributor cap.

Tires

Tires are one of the most important safety features on your car. Properly maintained tires will help your car drive and stop safely. Good tire care also allows the maximum life or mileage from the tires and the most MPG or fuel efficiency. Poorly maintained tires can cause the car to slide, go out of control, waste fuel, or cause pollution.

Proper tire inflation (Chapter 3) is very important regardless of the type of tires currently on your car. Rotating and balancing the tires (Chapter 5) can help the tires wear evenly. Wheel alignment (Chapter 7) is also important for safe handling and long tire life. When it comes time to shop for new tires, which type of tires should you buy for your car?

Replace Tires

Replace the tires when the wear bars begin to show or when the tire tread is 1/16 inch deep. It is best to buy four new tires at once. If, however, two of the old tires still have some tread on them, buy two new tires and continue to use the best two old tires (until they wear out). When shopping for new tires, ask for free lifetime rotation and balancing and a reduced price on a wheel alignment. Refer to Chapters 5 & 7 for more information.

Do not mix different sizes or types of tires on the same axle.

New Car Tires

Would you be surprised to find cheap tires on a new car? They are new tires and might look great and may even be manufactured by a well known company, but the quality is usually just average. Many car companies cut costs and increase profits by installing cheap tires on new cars. Therefore, do not be surprised if the tires on a new car do not handle very well or last very long. When you purchase replacement tires, look for good quality tires.

Shopping for tires according to a brand name or advertised specials does not guarantee you a good quality product.

Tire Quality

All tires are rated according to standard tests of quality. The results are imprinted onto the side of each tire, which allows you the rare opportunity of easily comparing the quality of different types and brands of tires. The standard ratings are: Temperature, Traction, and Treadwear.

Temperature

Temperature is rated A, B, and C; A is the best and C is the minimum. This rating reflects the ability of the tire to dissipate heat and avoid damage from fast driving or hot roads. Tires with a Temperature A rating will run cooler and should last longer.

Traction

Traction is also rated A, B, and C; A is the best and C is the minimum. This rating reflects the tire's traction on wet roads. Tires with a rating of Traction A will hold the road and be safer under normal driving conditions.

Treadwear

Treadwear is rated as a number, such as 100, 180, 210, or higher. A rating of 100 is standard. A 200 rated tire should last twice as long. Higher treadwear ratings indicate the tire is made with harder rubber and can be expected to last longer under similar driving conditions.

Tire Age

The Department Of Transportation (DOT) identification number will indicate where and when the tire was manufactured. A number ending with "374" would indicate that the tire was made during the 37th week of 1994. Do not buy tires that are over 1 year old, even if they look new. Old tires can develop problems and wear out quickly.

Speed Ratings

Tires are also rated for speed; however, unless your car wheels require the expensive tires or you plan on driving over 100 MPH, these expensive tires are not needed on your car. You can save money with good quality less expensive tires. Check the owners manual and be sure you purchase the correct size and type of tires for your car.

Radial Tires

Radial tires are a newer type of tire design, as compared to the older bias-ply or belted tires. Radial tires will provide superior traction, handling, fuel economy, and tire life compared to other types of tires. They may be more expensive to purchase, but the overall performance will be superior and the cost-per-mile should be much less.

Green Tires

New tire designs with improved rubber are now being marketed as "green tires." The tires are not green in color, but the extra mileage and longer lasting rubber are designed to reduce pollution and save you money.

Unfortunately, like most new inventions, these tires may be more expensive, but they are certainly worth your careful consideration.

Retread Tires

For many years, retreaded tires were very poor quality and the retread industry got a bad reputation. Recent improvements in the retread manufacturing process have produced outstanding results and retread tires are now used on most large trucks, planes, and buses. They may not be available in all sizes for passenger cars, but ask your local tire store for more information about retreads. They should offer similar performance at a much reduced cost. Using retreaded tires is a great way to recycle while you drive.

For most cars, look for radial tires with Temperature A, Traction A, and Treadwear of 200 (or higher).

New Tires On Your Old Car

You will be pleasantly surprised how well your "old car" drives with new tires. You will wonder why you attempted to get the last few miles out of those old tires. New tires are expensive, but not as expensive as a collision. Old worn tires are much more likely to have a blowout, go flat, or cause your car to skid.

Recycle Old Tires

Most tire stores charge a small fee to dispose of your old tires. Some tires can be recycled into retreads. Others can be used in some type of manufacturing process. Ask the tire store for details or call your local recycling center or retread manufacturer for more information. Do not keep old tires or allow them to be disposed of improperly. Old tires can collect water and breed mosquitoes, take up space in landfills, and cause dangerous pollution if they are burned.

Things To Do Every 4 Years

1. Replace the battery.
   Check the CCA - Cold Cranking Amps.

2. Replace the radiator cap.

3. Replace the radiator hoses & clamps.

4. Replace the thermostat.

5. Replace the water pump.

6. Replace the timing belt or check the timing chain.

7. Replace all engine belts.

8. Replace the rubber brake hoses.

9. Replace the fuel cap.

10. Test the fuel pump. Replace it, if necessary.

11. Replace the sparkplug wires.

12. Replace the tires, when necessary.
    Temperature A, Traction A, Treadwear 200+.

Additional items needed for your car:

Drive With Confidence

Owing a car requires many important decisions. For example, which type of car should you buy, will you do the maintenance yourself or find a mechanic, what should you do if you have a dispute over a repair, and how should you get rid of your car? This chapter provides some helpful tips to help you drive with confidence and have a long and happy relationship with your car.

Knowing more about your car will help you determine what service it needs or doesn't need. Regardless of the type of car you drive, car conservation will help you drive safer, farther, and reduce the overall cost-per-mile of owning a car.

Car conservation will help you drive with confidence.

Buying A Car

Buying a car can be a wonderful experience; it can also be a real headache. Driving around from car lot to car lot, checking the newspapers, reading consumer articles, taking test rides, fending off aggressive salespeople, talking to friends, the list seems to go on, and on, and on. This is a major financial decision and you want the best car at the least price. What can you do?

Slow Down

Take your time and do not let anyone rush you into making a quick decision. A common tactic used to sale cars is to make you believe that special deals are for a limited time and rush you into a bad decision. There are many good cars out there and if you miss one good deal, another one (possibly even better) will show up. What you need, what you want, and what you can afford may be very different and usually only careful consideration will help you sort out the facts from the fiction.

Budget

How much are you going to spend on the car? Make a budget and then stick with it. Better yet, spend only 90% of the money available, because there are other expenses, such as insurance, taxes, fuel, and maintenance, which are not covered in the purchase price of the car. If you buy more car than you can afford, hoping for a raise or the winning lottery ticket, you will regret it down the road. Overspending is one sure way to start out on the road to disaster.

Buy or Lease?

Should you buy or lease the car? Leasing is certainly becoming more popular and it does appeal to some people. With a lease you can usually drive a more expensive car with lower monthly payments. But do you really want to make car payments every month for the rest of your life? If you read the fine print on the lease agreement and calculate the numbers, you will find that leasing usually cost more (despite the lower payments) and buying a car will give you the most value.

New vs. Used

New cars are expensive. You will lose about 10% of the value of your new car as soon as you drive it home. In other words, if you change your mind after one month and decide to sell the car, you will lose over $1000. It is a perfectly good car, but it is not new.

Many people trade or sell their cars after about four or five years, when additional maintenance is needed. These cars are inexpensive to buy, but the warranty has expired and you will need to do some major maintenance very soon. Also, if the car is five years old, you have less time to drive it before it reaches 12 years or 250,000 miles.

The best value is often a used car between one and two years old with about 10,000 to 20,000 miles (except rental cars). These cars will be several thousand dollars less than similar new cars, but most likely still in good shape and still under warranty. Find out why the owner traded the car or talk with the previous owner to see if there were any problems with the car.

Check for recalls on any used car before you buy (see section on Recalls below).

First Year Models

Avoid all new models, or old models with major changes such as a new transmission or a new engine. Designing a good car is one thing, putting it into production is another. The first year of production is always difficult and these cars are much more likely to have flaws. Wait for the second or third year, when improvements have been implemented to correct the original design defects.

Gadgets

Avoid a car with lots of gadgets, such as power seats, power windows, power door locks, power mirrors, power this, and power that. These items are convenient and fun to use, but when they break they can be very expensive and hard to repair. Certainly you do not want to drive around with the seat out of position or get locked out of your car on a cold winter night. Expensive car stereos and electronic accessories, including alarms, may invite a thief to break into your car.

Independent Inspection

If you are buying a car over three years old, have the car inspected by an independent mechanic of your choice who has experience with this type of car. The $50 to $100 fee for a written report of both the current condition and upcoming maintenance needs is a wise investment. A four-year-old car may be in good shape, but within a year or two you may need to spend over a thousand dollars in maintenance and repairs. Most mechanics will find something *wrong* with any car. This does not necessarily indicate you should not buy the car, but you should use this information to negotiate a lower price for the car. Also, if you buy the car and it immediately has problems, you have some leverage with the mechanic.

Recalls

Each year thousands of cars are recalled for safety problems or design defects. You can find out if your car, or the car you intend to buy, has been recalled by calling **1-800-424-9393.** The Auto Safety Hotline is sponsored by the National Highway Traffic Safety Administration. Follow the recorded messages to leave the make, model, and year of the car, and your name and address. A free report about recall information will be mailed to you. Be sure any recall items have been corrected before you buy the car.

Call 1-800-424-9393 to check on recalls or report a safety problem with your car.

Do-It-Yourself Maintenance

Can you do the maintenance on your own car? Yes, if you have a little mechanical ability and the following: *parts, tools, and a shop manual.* Most maintenance items do not require special tools or training, but you should follow the steps outlined in the shop manual to avoid personal injuries or damage to the car. The high tech computers and electronic equipment usually operate for many years without adjustments or repairs, if you change the fluids and filters and basic maintenance parts regularly. Leave the complex tasks, such as air conditioning service, electronic engine diagnostic work, or wheel alignments to the experienced professionals.

Tools

Every car should have a basic tool kit, as discussed in Chapter 3. If, however, you plan to do the maintenance for the car, you may need some additional tools. Always use good quality tools and use the right tool for the job. Cheap tools might slip or break and cause an injury or car damage. Good quality tools with a lifetime guarantee are available from hardware or auto parts stores. Look for special sales for the best value. An assortment of car care tools for dong basic preventive maintenance will cost about $100 to $250.

Help

If you are attempting a job for the first time, or are unsure how to do a particular maintenance item, ask for help. Some maintenance jobs require two people and it is always helpful and safer to have someone to assist you. Use the shop manual and follow the recommendations carefully. Many community colleges or adult education centers offer basic car care classes where you can learn how to safely maintain your car. Write or call CoNation for other available books, videos, and computer programs about car repair.

Shop Manual

A shop manual describes the proper repair and maintenance for your particular car. Shop manuals are available at your local library, auto store, or the dealership. Although most of the information in the shop manual is very technical (for example, how to rebuild the engine or transmission), the basic maintenance procedures are also covered with step-by-step instructions and many helpful photos or diagrams.

Finding A Mechanic

Once you own a car, it is up to you to maintain it in safe reliable condition. If you do not have the time (or talent) to do the maintenance yourself, find a mechanic. Do not wait until the car breaks down or develops a problem to start looking for a mechanic. Find a mechanic now.

Check the phone book under *Automobile Repair.* Ask your friends or co-workers to recommend a mechanic or shop and if the service is reliable. Ask someone who drives a similar type car where they have found good mechanics. Once you find a shop you like, call the local Better Business Bureau to see if any unresolved complaints are registered with the shop.

ASE Certification

ASE certification is the Automotive Service Excellence voluntary testing program. Mechanics can be certified in different areas of car repair, such as brakes, engine, transmissions, electrical, heating & A/C, etc. The certification belongs to the mechanic, not the shop; however, shops usually advertise when they employ ASE certified technicians. A mechanic certified in all areas is considered a Master Automobile Technician. Be sure the mechanic working on your car is the one with the proper ASE certification for the job.

Work With The Repair Shop

Follow these easy steps to get good service from the dealership or repair shop and avoid the headaches of delays and misunderstandings.

1. Whenever possible, make an appointment. If you must change your plans for some reason, notify the shop immediately.

2. Give a written note to the service manager when you take your car in for service. Include your name, address, phone number, the make, model, color of your car, plus the VIN (Vehicle Identification Number) and license plate numbers. Describe the work you need done. If you do not know what the problem is, describe the symptoms as completely as possible. Keep a copy of this note for your records.

3. After inspecting your car, the service manager or mechanic should be able to tell you the repairs needed, or a test which will determine the exact problem. Either way, get a written estimate of the time and cost for the work, or test, before you leave.

4. If the shop does not call you, check on the progress of the work after the allotted time. If additional repairs are needed, get an estimate of the time and cost involved. Make a written note about telephone calls, indicating the time, person, and items discussed.

5. When you pick up the car, carefully review the bill. It should include a description of the car, mileage, date, and work done. Review the list of work requested to be sure all items were fixed. Separate totals for parts and labor should be clearly indicated. Check the bill for any unauthorized or miscellaneous charges and request a clear explanation.

6. Inspect the car carefully and go for a test drive. Be sure the appropriate work was done and no other damage or problems exist. If you notice a problem after leaving the shop, return to the shop immediately or start over with step #1.

Special Repairs

Most general repair shops do a good job at basic maintenance. Because of the increasing complexity of car design and high cost of specialized tools, some shops deal only with certain repairs or certain types of cars. It is not unusual for you to need four different mechanics: one for basic service (oil changes), one for transmission service, one for tires, brakes, suspension, and one for engines or complex repairs. Of course, you could go to the dealership for any repair, but the cost of both parts and labor is usually much higher and the quality of the service is not always good.

Resolving Car Problems

The most important step in resolving a car problem takes place before the problem arises. Keep a written record or logbook, as described in Chapter 1, of any maintenance and repair done to your car. This applies to work done by the dealership, local mechanic, or you. In case of a dispute, you need written evidence of dates, mileage, and work done. You should also keep receipts, but you can get a copy of the receipt easily if you know the date the work was done and the receipt (invoice) number.

Be Patient

Patience helps to resolve disputes. Many service facilities will attempt to delay or frustrate the process, hoping you will give up and either go somewhere else or pay for additional repairs yourself. Resolving repair disputes is not easy, but if you are persistent the problem will eventually be fixed.

Step One

After a repair job, if either the original problem remains or another problem arises, give the shop another chance to fix it. Of course, there should be no additional charges for work which was not done properly the first time. Get another work order or invoice to indicate the additional work was done at no charge.

Step Two

If the problem still is not fixed, write a letter to the shop owner or manager. Describe the problem as clearly as possible and the work done. Include copies of the first two work orders. Indicate that you are willing to give them a final opportunity to fix the problem. Send the letter (return receipt requested) and arrange a final appointment.

Step Three

If the problem still is not fixed, either the repair facility does not know how to fix it or is unwilling to fix it. Your next step may depend on the type of repair shop you are dealing with. If the repair shop is part of a nationwide facility or dealership, you should contact the regional or national office. Call to find out who handles these types of complaints and discuss the situation with them. Perhaps you can negotiate for another shop in your area to fix the problem.

If the repair shop is privately owned, your options are more limited. You might discuss the situation with the owner, but if the written letter did not get the owner's attention, more dialogue is unlikely to succeed.

Step Four

Finally, the only choice you may have is to pursue legal action or go somewhere else. Either choice is unpleasant and unfortunate. Hopefully, you will never arrive at this situation. If you do seek legal action, find an attorney who specializes in automotive law and the "lemon laws." It could be that poor design, not faulty repairs, is responsible for the problem(s). Several arbitration programs are available to mediate automobile disputes. For more information about legal action, contact the local office of the Federal Trade Commission or get a copy of <u>The Lemon Book</u>.

Selling A Car

Selling a used car is not easy. When a person can go to the dealership and finance a brand new car with only a small down payment, they are unlikely to pay several thousand dollars for a used car. Many people are afraid to buy a used car; they feel something must be wrong with it, or you would not want to sell it.

If you do sell your car to someone, never take a personal check; insist on cash or money order.

What can you do to make a used car more attractive to a buyer? First, be open about your reason for selling the car. Is it too big, too small, or do you just want a different car? There are many good reasons to sell a car. You should also wash and clean the car inside and out. Vacuum the carpets and clean out the glove compartment. Some shops will professionally clean your car for under $100. Few people will buy a dirty car. Finally, be sure the car runs safely. Check the brakes, suspension, engine, and transmission. If any problems are found, either fix them or tell the buyer about the problems. Show the logbook to the buyer and demonstrate that you have taken good care of the car.

Book Value

The book value refers to one of the standard reference books which provides the approximate value of any used car. These books are available at bookstores, news stands, or libraries. Find the make, model, and year of the car. Then estimate if the car is in good, fair, or poor condition to determine the approximate value. Adjust the price for certain options, such as air conditioning, power options, or other features. The book value is only a guide; your car is actually worth what someone will give you for it.

Trade In

Of course, you may want to avoid the hassles and inconvenience of selling the car by simply offering it as a trade-in on your next car. Most car dealers will accept any type of car in any condition as a trade-in; however, the trade-in value is going to be much less than the retail value. You should negotiate the lowest possible price on the new car (without a trade-in), and then negotiate the highest possible price of your old car as a trade-in. Otherwise, the dealer might not offer the best selling price.

Negotiate the lowest possible price on the new car (without the trade-in), then negotiate the highest possible value on the trade-in of the old car.

Afterword

If you want your car to last a long time, learn to be a car conservationist. Safe driving habits and good car care are the keys to a long and happy relationship with your car. It is not which type of car you drive, but how you drive and how you maintain your car that will save you thousands of dollars in unwanted repairs. Now that you know the easy ways to keep your car running great, you can drive with confidence.

Remember that the guidelines in the book are for normal driving conditions of between 1000 and 1500 miles per month. If you are driving more or less each month, you may want to adjust your maintenance schedule accordingly. However, do not postpone needed maintenance until something major breaks and causes a roadside breakdown or expensive repair. Car conservation is safe, cost effective car care which will keep your car running efficiently for many, many years.

To learn more about how your car operates and the keys to the mechanical mysteries, write to CoNation Publications for a complete list of car care books, audio, video, and computer programs.

Even if you never plan to repair your own car, just knowing more about how it works can help you communicate effectively with a mechanic.

I would like to thank all those who contributed ideas, comments, and suggestions about this book. Without your help and encouragement, **The Green Machine** would not exist.

Thank you for taking the time to read this book and I sincerely hope you will find it helpful as you become a car conservationist and learn to drive a *Green Machine.* If you have a comment or question about your car, send it to the Car Care Professor c/o CoNation Publications or via CompuServe.

Drive Safely

Drive With Confidence

Drive Green !

Jim Gaston
the Car Care Professor

CompuServe #71732.471

**CoNation Publications
703-G Ninth Street
Durham NC 27705**

Phone / FAX (919) 477-5397

GLOSSARY

A

ABS - Anti-lock Brake System prevents the front wheels from locking during sudden stops and allows you to steer the car during sudden stops.

A/C - Air Conditioning. See also alternating current.

Air Cleaner - the metal container which holds the air filter.

Air Filter - the replaceable part inside the air cleaner which
removes dirt and dust from the air entering the engine.

Air Pressure Gauge - measures the amount of air inside the tires. PSI = Pounds per Square Inch.

A.I.R. Pump - Air Injection Reaction pump is part of the exhaust gas emission controls.

Alternating Current - electricity reversing directions (as opposed to flowing in one direction). See direct current.

Alternator - produces electricity needed to charge the battery and operate the accessories in the car.

Ampere - AMP - amount of electric current or power.

Antifreeze - see coolant.

ATF - See Automatic Transmission Fluid.

Automatic Transmission Fluid - hydraulic fluid in the automatic transmission and some power steering systems.

B

Ball Joint - flexible connection on the steering or suspension system. See tie rod.

Battery - a plastic box containing metal plates in acid and water. Most automotive batteries provides electrical power at 12 Volts.

Belt - a flexible rubber belt on the engine. See timing belt.

Bearing - the part used to reduce friction between two moving parts. Bearings are found inside the engine, transmission, or near each wheel.

Black Box - any electronic device which cannot be adjusted or repaired; it must be replaced when damaged.

Bleeding - removing air bubbles from the hydraulic system.

Book Value - Calculating the standard cost of a used car, based on the age, mileage, and condition of the car. Most libraries and book stores have these reference books.

Boot - a rubber cover used to keep out dirt and water.

Brake Fluid - a special fluid used in the brake (or clutch) system.

Brake Pads - the replaceable part of the brake which is pressed against a rotating metal surface to slow down or stop the car. Also called brake shoes. See disc and drum brakes.

Bushing - a rubber part which absorbs vibrations and reduces rattles.

C

Caliper - the part of the disc brake which pushes the brake pads against the rotating disc.

Camber - a measurement of the wheel alignment.

Carburetor - a method of mixing the gasoline with air so it can be burned inside the engine. See fuel injection.

Caster - a measurement of the wheel alignment.

Catalytic Converter - a part of the exhaust system used reduce harmful pollution.

CCA - see cold cranking amps.

Centrifugal Advance - adjusting the timing of the engine with small rotating weights. See vacuum advance.

Choke - used to start a cold engine. The choke limits the air entering the engine and produces a richer (more fuel) mixture.

Clutch - the connection between the engine and transmission.

Coil - boost the low battery voltage (12 volts) to a high voltage (20,000 volts) needed for the sparkplugs.

Cold Cranking Amps - the amount of electrical power (amps) a battery can deliver when it is at 0°F or -18°C.

Compression Test - an easy way to check the internal condition of an engine. Low compression usually indicates major engine repairs are needed.

Coolant - chemical mixed with water to make radiator fluid. The coolant, or anti-freeze, lubricates the cooling system, prevents rust, and helps prevent overheating and freezing.

Criss-Cross - a method of tightening opposite lug nuts to insure that the wheel is tighten evenly and correctly.

C.V. Joint - Constant Velocity Joint - the flexible connection on the ends of a drive shaft. See universal joint.

CW - Clock Wise - turning to the RIGHT or the direction a clock hand moves. The normal way to tighten a screw or bolt.

CCW - Counter Clock Wise - turning to the LEFT or the opposite direction a clock hand moves to loosen parts.

D

Dead Battery - a battery without adequate power to start the engine.

DC - See direct current.

Dieseling - an engine which continues to run after the key switch is turned to OFF.

Differential - part of the transmission which allows the wheels to turn smoothly in a curve.

Dipstick - used to measure a fluid level.

Direct Current - electrical power flowing in only one direction, such as a battery. See alternating current.

Disc Brake - a flat rotating disc (rotor) with a stationary caliper and flat brake pads. Normally used on the front wheels.

Distributor Cap - the removable top part of the distributor where the spark plugs wires are attached.

Down Shifting - slowing the car or increasing the engine speed by shifting into a lower gear.

Drive Train - parts of the car located between the engine and the drive wheels: clutch, transmission, differential, drive shafts, and universal (or CV) joints.

Drum Brake - a curved rotating drum with a stationary wheel cylinder and curved brake pads. Normally used on the rear wheels where the parking brake is attached.

E

EGR - see Exhaust Gas Recirculating Valve

Electrical System Indicators - battery warning light, ammeter, or voltmeter.

Electronic Ignition System - a more expensive, but reliable, type of ignition system that does not use points or condensers. See black box.

Engine Temperature Indicators - the temperature gauge or temperature warning light used to indicate the engine temperature.

Exhaust Gas Recirculating Valve - part of the emission controls needed to reduce air pollution.

Expansion Tank - the reservoir for excess radiator fluid.

Evaporator - a small radiator under the dashboard needed for the A/C system.

F

Fading - when the brakes (drum) get very hot and cannot stop the car during heavy use.

Fan - forces air through the radiator to cool the radiator fluid and keep the engine from overheating.

Float - Float Valve - parts inside the carburetor used to regulate the flow of gasoline to the engine.

Flooding - too much fuel (or not enough air) at the engine, which can prevent the engine from starting.

Four Wheel Drive - (4WD) - using all four wheels for extra traction to pull or push the car.

Free Play - see play.

Friction - resistance to motion between two surfaces. Oil is used inside the engine to reduce friction and heat.

Front Wheel Drive - (FWD) - using the front wheels to the pull the car.

Fuel-Air Mixture - the mixture burned inside the engine to produce the power needed to turn the engine and move the car.

Fuel Filter - removes dirt and water from the fuel before it enters the engine.

Fuel Injection - mixing the fuel and air by squirting fuel directly into the engine. Used on both gasoline and diesel engines. Used instead of a carburetor.

Fuel Pedal - controls the power and speed of the engine.

Fuel Pump - a small pump needed to move the fuel from the tank to the engine. The fuel pump may be electric (in the tank) or mechanical (on the engine).

Fuse - the "weak-link" to protect the electrical system from excessive power.

Fuse Box - a central location for the fuses.

Fusible Link - a small piece of wire or metal placed in a main circuit which melts and acts like a main fuse.

G

Gap - the distance between the electrodes on a sparkplug as measured with a round gauge.

Gasket - a soft material used to form an airtight seal between two surfaces.

Gears - part of the transmission needed for increasing the speed of the car.

Glow Plugs - needed to start a cold diesel engine.

Grease - a very thick lubricant used on some bearings and the suspension.

Grease Fitting - is where a grease gun can be attached to add grease. See ball joint.

Grease Gun - a tool used to inject grease into grease fittings.

Ground - any metal part of the car. One battery terminal (normally the NEG) is connected to the metal frame to allow the electrical power to make a complete circuit.

H

Head Gasket - the seal between the engine block and cylinder head. A "blown" head gasket will cause low compression and loss of oil or coolant.

Horsepower - measurement of the power produced by the engine. See torque.

Hose Clamps - the metal bands which hold the rubber hoses in place and prevent leaks.

HP - See horsepower.

Hydraulic - using fluid pressure to transmit a force. See bleeding.

Hydroplaning - a loss of traction when the car is driven very fast on wet roads.

I

Idle - the minimum operating speed of the engine.

Ignition - producing a spark to ignite the fuel-air mixture inside the engine.

Insert - the rubber part of the windshield wiper blade.

J

Jack - a tool used to lift the car when changing a flat tire.

Jack Stand - a special tool designed to support the weight of the car.

Jumper Cables - the large wires with clamps at both ends used to connect a two batteries during a jump-start.

Jump-Start - connecting two batteries together to start a car with a "dead" battery.

K

Key Switch - operates the starter motor and the accessories.

Knock - the sound made by the engine when the fuel-air mixture is not burning properly. See octane.

KPH - Kilometers Per Hour - a measure of the speed of the car. See speedometer, MPH, and RPM.

L

Leaf Springs - Long flat bars of metal fastened together to absorb bumps. Most commonly used on rear wheels of larger cars or trucks.

Lean - a mixture containing more air (less fuel).

Linkage - any system of cables, levers, springs, and brackets. See fuel pedal.

Lubrication - reducing the friction between moving parts in order to extend the life and performance of the car.

Lug Nuts - the bolts holding the wheel onto the axle.

Lug Wrench - see tire tool.

M

Manifold - a set of pipes used to move gases from on place to another. For example: intake manifold or exhaust manifold.

Master Cylinder - see primary cylinder.

MPG - Miles Per Gallon - the number of miles a car can drive on one gallon of fuel.

MPH -Miles Per Hour - measurement of the speed of the car. See KPH, RPM.

Motor Mounts - a special large bushing holding the engine or transmission to the frame of the car.

Muffler - part of the exhaust system used to reduce noise.

Multi-Grade Oil - oil with special additives to change the thickness (or weight) at various temperatures. For example: 10W40 or 5W30 oils are multi-grade or multi-weight oils.

N

Negative Ground - when the NEGative battery terminal is connected to the metal frame or engine.

NEGative - one of the terminals on the battery (-).

O

Octane - a measurement of the "anti-knock" ability of fuels. The higher octane fuel is more resistant to knocking, but does not offer more power, better cleaning, or additional performance.

Odometer - measures the distance the car has driven.

OEM - Original Equipment of the Manufacturer or dealership parts.

Oil Filter - removes dirt and impurities from the engine oil.

Oil Pressure Indicators - the oil warning light or pressure gauge.

Oil Pan - bottom part of the engine where oil is held.

Overdrive - an extra gear in the transmission to allow the engine to turn slower at highway speeds for additional fuel economy.

Oxygen Sensor - part of the emission controls that measurers the exhaust gases to determine if the fuel-air mixture is too lean or rich.

P

Parking Brake - brake system used to hold the car when parked.

PCV - see positive crankcase ventilation.

Play - the small distance the steering wheel can be moved without causing the front tires to move, or a pedal can moved without causing the system to operate.

Points - part of the standard ignition system which needs to be replaced often. See electronic ignition system.

POSitive - one of the terminals on the battery (+).

Positive Crankcase Ventilation - part of the emission controls used to reduce harmful emission from the engine.

Power Brakes - using vacuum (suction) from the engine to reduce the amount of force needed to operate the brake pedal.

Power Steering - using a small hydraulic pump to reduce the force needed to turn the steering wheel.

Power Train - parts of the car that transmit the power from the engine to the wheels.

Pounds per Square Inch - PSI - a measure of pressure, such as the air in the tires or oil pressure.

Pressure Cap - see radiator cap.

Primary Cylinder - the part of the hydraulic system where the force (from the foot pedal) is applied. See secondary cylinder.

PSI - see pound per square inch.

Q

Quick Charge - charging a car battery in a short time, which can damage the battery. See trickle charge.

R

Rack & Pinion - a type of steering system.

Radial Tire - a tire which can improve handling ability and fuel economy of the car.

Radiator - used to transfer heat from the fluid to the air. Sometimes called a cooler.

Radiator Cap - is the part on the top of the radiator which regulates the pressure inside the radiator.

Radiator Fan - is used to blow air through the radiator.

Rebuilt - a used part which has been repaired and tested.

Remanufactured - a used part which has been completely disassembled, cleaned, repaired, and tested to "like-new" condition.

Redline - the maximum speed of the engine.

Rotations Per Minute - RPM - is the speed which the parts inside the engine are turning. See MPH, KPH.

Rotor - the part under the distributor cap which turns or the flat metal part of the disc brake.

RPM - see rotations per minute.

S

Secondary Cylinder - responds to the force applied at the primary cylinder. See primary cylinder and hydraulic.

Self Adjusters - the device on rear brakes used to automatically adjust the brake pads.

Sending Unit - the part which "sends" information to the dashboard gauge/light or computer.

Shock Absorber - a part of the suspension used to absorb vibrations and reduce excessive bouncing of the springs.

Shop Manual - the book containing complete instruction about all repairs and maintenance for a car.

Short Circuit - an alternate path (or circuit) in the electrical system which can damage the wires and cause an electrical fire.

Spark Advance - adjusting the distributor (timing) while the engine is running to allow smooth engine operation at all speeds.

Spark Plug - the part of a gasoline engine that produces the spark needed to ignite the fuel-air mixture inside the engine.

Speedometer - the instrument used to measure the speed of the car in MPH or KPH. See tachometer.

Springs - flexible metal parts of the suspension system which support the weight of the car.

Standard Ignition System - older ignition system which uses points and condenser. See electronic ignition system.

Starter - a powerful electric motor needed to turn the parts inside the engine until the fuel-air starts to burn.

Steering System - the parts of the car that allow the steering wheel to control the position of the front wheels.

Strut - a special suspension system where the shock absorber is located inside the coil spring.

Supercharger - is turned by an engine belt and forces air into the engine to produce more power, but decreases fuel economy. See turbocharger.

Suspension System - the parts of the car that support the weight of the car and provide a smooth ride.

Synthetic Oil - special more expensive oil made from ultra refined petroleum or non-petroleum products.

T

Tachometer - measures the engine speed or how fast parts inside the engine are turning in RPMs. See speedometer.

TDC - see Top Dead Center

Thermostat - is used to regulate the engine temperature.

Tie Rod - part of the steering system. Ball joints are located on the end of the tie rod.

Timing - adjustments made to the ignition system to allow the sparkplugs to operate at the proper time.

Timing Belt - the belt (or chain) inside the engine used to control the engine valves. See valves.

Timing Light - tool used to check or adjust the engine timing.

Tire Tool - the tool used to remove lug nuts. See lug wrench.

Tire Valve - where air is added to the tire and the air pressure is checked.

Tire - the rubber part of the wheel.

Toe-In - Toe-Out - adjustments of the wheel alignment.

Top Dead Center - when the cylinder is at the top position in the engine. TDC is often used to adjust the engine timing.

Torque - a measure of the twisting force. See horsepower.

Torque Converter - part of the automatic transmission which acts like a clutch. See clutch.

Torque Wrench - a tool used to precisely tighten a part.

Traction - the ability of the wheels to grip the road surface and avoid skidding or sliding.

Trans-axle - a combination transmission and differential (or axle) used on many front wheel drive cars.

Tread Wear Indicator - the rubber section molded into the tire to indicates the minimum safe tread.

Trickle Charge - charging the battery slowly to avoid damage to the battery.

Tune-up - adjustments to the engine so that it will start easily, run smoothly, and have normal fuel economy (MPG).

Turbocharger - is turned by exhaust gases leaving the engine and increases the fuel economy and performance of the engine. See supercharger.

Turn - spinning the brake drum or rotor to remove small scratches and produce a very smooth surface.

U

Undercoat - a protective coating applied underneath the car to help prevent rust.

Universal Joint - the flexible connections on the ends of the drive shaft. Also called a CV Joint or Constant Velocity Joint.

V

Vacuum - suction caused by the movement of parts inside the engine.

Vacuum Advance- adjusting the timing of the engine with vacuum from the engine. See centrifugal advance.

Vacuum Gauge - the instrument used to measure the amount of suction produced by the engine.

Valves - parts inside the engine which allow the fuel-air mixture to enter and the exhaust gases to exit. See timing belt.

Vapor Lock - when the fuel lines are very hot and small bubbles form inside the fuel pump. This can cause the engine to stop.

Viscosity - a measure of the thickness of oil. Higher viscosity means a thicker oil.

Voltage Regulator - controls the electricity produced by the alternator.

W

Warning Light - a small light on the dashboard which indicates an important condition.

Water Pump - circulates the radiator fluid between the engine and radiator.

Water Separator - a special filter on a diesel engine used to remove water from the fuel supply.

Wear-Bars - see tread wear indicators.

Wheel - the rubber tire and metal rim assembly.

Wheel Alignment - the exact position of the tires needed for proper handling, even tread wear and good fuel economy.

Wheel Cylinder - see secondary cylinder.

Wiring Diagram - a drawing of all the wires and electrical devices found in the shop manual.

Wiring Harness - the collection of wires used to transmit electrical power.

Index

A

B

C

D

E

F

Fuel
>injector cleaning 117
>oxygenated 100
>pedal 10, 30
>pump 87, 132
>tank 15

G

Gadgets 144
Gauge air pressure 46
Gauges 26

H

Head restraint 7
Headlights 25
Heater 5, 53
Horn 27
Hose clamps 62, 124
Hoses
>brake 130
>radiator 62

I

Idle speed 96

K

L

M

O

S

T

V

W

Maintenance Logbook

Name

Address

City   **ZIP**

Phone

Year

Make / Model

VIN
(Vehicle Identification Number)

License Number

Insurance Policy Number

Insurance Phone

Doctor Phone

Relative Phone

Mechanic Phone

Order a **Car Care Logbook** *for a friend.*
Use the **ORDER FORM** *at the back of this*
book or contact CoNation Publications.

Date	Destination / Purpose / Repair

Odometer		Miles	Expenses	Driver
Begin	End		$ Amount	Invoice #

Date	Destination / Purpose / Repair

Odometer		Miles	Expenses	Driver
Begin	End		$ Amount	Invoice #

Date	Destination / Purpose / Repair

Odometer		Miles	Expenses	Driver
Begin	End		$ Amount	Invoice #

Order Form

Order Form

___ **The Green Machine**   **$12.95**

___ **Car Care Logbook**   **$ 4.95**

___ **Drive Green**   **$ 4.95**

TOTAL _____

For FREE information about all the books, audio tapes, and computer programs on car conservation offered by CoNation Publications, CALL, FAX, or WRITE today!

Full Refund If Not Completely Satisfied

NC Residents add Sales Tax
FREE Shipping to USA / Canada
Faster AIR MAIL shipping: Add $2.95 per order

Send Your Check or Money Order To:

CoNation Publications
703-G Ninth Street
Durham NC 27705

(919) 477-5397

Drive Green